For all those who freed themselves
by cutting the rope.

Strange Fruit

Volume I

Uncelebrated Narratives from Black History

words and pictures by
Joel Christian Gill

Library of Congress Cataloging-in-Publication Data

Gill, Joel Christian.
Uncelebrated narratives from Black history / words and pictures by Joel Christian Gill;
foreword by Henry Louis Gates, Jr.

pages cm -- (Strange fruit ; volume 1)
Summary: "Strange Fruit, Volume I, Uncelebrated narratives from Black history is a collection of stories from African American history that exemplifies success in the face of great adversity. This unique graphic anthology offers historical and cultural commentary on nine uncelebrated heroes whose stories are not often found in history books. Among the stories included are: Henry 'Box' Brown, who escaped from slavery by mailing himself to Philadelphia; Alexander Crummel and the Noyes Academy, the first integrated school in America, established in the 1830s; Marshall 'Major' Taylor, a.k.a. the Black Cyclone, the first Black champion in any sport; and Bass Reeves, the most successful lawman in the Old West. Written and illustrated by Joel Christian Gill, the diverse art beautifully captures the spirit of each remarkable individual and opens a window into an important part of American history"-- Provided by publisher.

Audience: Age 12 to 18.
ISBN 978-1-938486-29-6 (paperback)
1. African Americans--Biography--Juvenile literature. 2. African Americans--Biography--Comic books, strips, etc. 3. Heroes--United States--Biography--Juvenile literature. 4. Heroes--United States--Biography--Comic books, strips, etc. 5. African Americans--History--Anecdotes--Juvenile literature. 6. African Americans--History--Anecdotes--Comic books, strips, etc. 7. Graphic novels. I. Title.
E185.96.G54 2014
973.04960730092'2--dc23
[B]

2014010803

Printed in the United States
0 9 8 7 6 5 4 3 2 1

Fulcrum Publishing
4690 Table Mountain Dr., Ste. 100
Golden, CO 80403
800-992-2908 • 303-277-1623
www.fulcrumbooks.com

Contents

Why Strange Fruit?

I had lived in the South all my life, but in 2002, my family and I moved to Boston so I could go to grad school at Boston University. I was terrified. I was not sure what to expect. After all, I'd grown up in a small town in Virginia. At 13 I moved to a small city, but it was nothing like Boston. After the arduous 13-hour journey, my wife and I moved our three daughters and infant son into our third-story walk-up.

A few weeks later, I took a trip with my MFA painting class to the Museum of Fine Arts, where I struck up a conversation with a security guard while waiting to get into an exhibit. He told me that he was born and raised in Boston but would never root for the Red Sox. He then began to tell me of racism by the Red Sox back in the day – race riots and neighborhoods where black men were still not welcome. Needless to say, I was dumbfounded. I had lived in a town where there was a Ku Klux Klan march when I was in third grade and where there was a famous "lynching tree." Yet I rode my bike all over the place and was never afraid. Now, here I was being advised to stay out of certain neighborhoods. I did not see discrimination during the two years I lived in Boston, but I steered clear of the neighborhoods I'd been warned about.

After our time in Boston, my family and I moved back to the South. I was happy to be home. I realized that I was a southerner down to the bones. As an undergrad, I had researched some ideas for paintings based on lynching photographs. Now, I felt, was the time to follow through. I listened to the song "Strange Fruit" by Billie Holiday, based on the poem by Abel Meeropol, and I decided to call my paintings "Strange Fruit Harvested: He Cut the Rope," showing me with a noose around my neck, holding the frayed end. I was trying to say that I was in some ways freed from the fear that had plagued my father and grandfather. However, I also wanted to convey that because the rope was still there, we still had a ways to go.

What does this have to do with black history, you might ask? At this show, a good friend told me that my paintings were trying hard to tell a story, but they were coming up short. I had originally gone to school because I wanted to learn to draw comics, and with that one comment, I had come full circle. I started making comics.

I wanted to tell stories – sometimes great and sometimes tragic – of other people who were also able to "cut the rope." So, I began to research and draw comics about obscure black history. I looked for stories of people who were not in mainstream history books. I wanted to tell stories that people had not heard. I began finding all sorts of material. I drew my first story and was ready to present it to the world. But what to call it? I knew I wanted to tell a lot of these stories in my self-published periodic mini-comics, so I wanted to name it something in keeping with those. I realized that this was close to the work I had done before, so I went with the same title: "Strange Fruit."

Strange Fruit: Uncelebrated Narratives from Black History, Volume 1 tells stories of people who, in spite of the "Strange Fruit" society where they lived, liberated themselves from the magnolia trees and tried to do something amazing. Whether it was escaping from slavery in a box or chasing down outlaws, these people epitomized cutting the rope. Billie Holiday sang about the time in which she lived. These stories are about amazing people during those times who, in many ways, cut their own rope.

Joel Christian Gill

Foreword

In her rendering of the song "Strange Fruit," first lady of the blues Billie Holiday painted, with her voice, gruesome images of African American people "hangin' from the poplar trees" of the Jim Crow South in a system of crude, and cruel, injustice well outside the law. No one who has heard her Depression-era recording can forget the feeling of Abel Meeropol's lyrics – and Holiday's anguished delivery of them – working their way up the spine. In his breakthrough graphic novel, gifted artist and storyteller Joel Christian Gill paints for us a different kind of "Strange Fruit": not the unspeakable crimes against humanity inflicted on black Americans throughout our history, but the unspoken heroes of our past, dangling outside an educational system, which, beyond highlighting the "greatest hits" of Black History Month, leaves too many children to strive without steeping them in the stories of their ancestors who succeeded against the steepest of odds.

That is the inspiration of Gill's graphic novel – less to teach our young than to excite them to be curious and teach themselves. Some, I know, are experimenting with jazz and hip-hop music to facilitate classroom learning. Others are reaching kids through hands-on or site-based experiences, not to mention sports. Still others are working hard to keep the conversation going after church on Sunday and at the dinner table. My bailiwick is scholarship and making documentary films. Now, Joel Christian Gill is joining the effort by leveraging his dazzling artistic talents to enliven those who typically receive only encyclopedic treatment. And the pictures he paints are cleverly revealing, at times irreverent, and always entertaining.

They are part of a storytelling tradition that is indelible to the African American experience, and has been since the days when it was against the law for slaves to be taught to read and write. A number of them did anyway, breaking the rules to force the country to rewrite them. Many more coped within the confines of race by playing the dozens, riffing, scratching, and signifying the tropes and tales that their families and neighbors had been passing down as oral history for generations.

Gill's *Strange Fruit* is in that venerable tradition, combining the best of the sleuthing historian's search for buried bones of the past with a folklorist's instinct for shrouding history in legend. Filling the pages of his book are brilliant images and pithy commentary that I'm sure will stoke children's curiosity to go to the local library to find out more, much the same way American schoolchildren for years have received their introduction to George Washington through the legend of his cherry tree, Abraham Lincoln by way of a log cabin, and Ben Franklin via kite and key. Gill's figures fit within that convention but with a black twist: I doubt many will have heard of all the names in this book, but after following the stories box by box, they will become part of the stories you tell on holidays, at the barbershop, or perhaps thinking of ideas for that next book report: Henry "Box" Brown, Richard Potter, Theophilus Thompson, Benjamin Darling, Alexander Crummell, Marshall Taylor, Spotswood Rice, Bass Reeves. Historians like me write about characters like these for a living; Gill animates them with his pen.

By the time I finished reading *Strange Fruit*, I thought, let the comic-book sellers have their mythic superheroes; through Joel Christian Gill, we can have our own. But, instead of flying around in capes or spinning webs, the superheroes in *Strange Fruit* are extraordinary-ordinary black folks making "a way out of no way." The difference: they really lived.

When Billie Holiday first performed "Strange Fruit" in the late 1930s, it wasn't uncommon for African Americans to be told they didn't have a history, at least one worth studying. I applaud Joel Christian Gill for using his art to remind rising generations that they do. Obviously, we won't be able to close the curriculum gap in our nation's schools with one book, as remarkable as it is; but by publishing our history in a form that is hip and fun, Joel Christian Gill promises to cut through the noise with black superheroes who defined our history in ways that will inspire our children and grandchildren to brave – and cross over – the rivers of the future.

Henry Louis Gates, Jr.
Alphonse Fletcher University Professor
Harvard University
Cambridge, Massachusetts
Spring 2014

UNNNN UHHH!!
Around 1815, in a small county outside of Richmond, Virginia, a boy was born into slavery.
Come now, a lil' bit mo'.

He was born the property of the Browns, so he became Henry Brown. Henry's bed was a box.
Lord have mercy!

Irony, noun: often confused with coincidence in situations where something happens that seems to foreshadow future events.

Out-of-the-Box Thinking
Henry BOX Brown
To say that Henry hated being a slave was an understatement.
THIS STINKS.
WHIP!

You fixin' to make me some money, boy.
Henry's master had devised a plan.

Henry was shipped off to a tobacco factory.
THIS STINKS.
To say that Henry hated the factory would, again, be an understatement.

After a while, Henry tried to see the silver lining in the cloud that hung over him.

Lucky for Henry, that silver lining had a name: Nancy.

Henry and Nancy fell in love, and for once in his life...

This does not stink!

After jumping the broom into the land of matrimony, Henry and Nancy started working on a family.

Slaves always work hard!

All in a day's work!

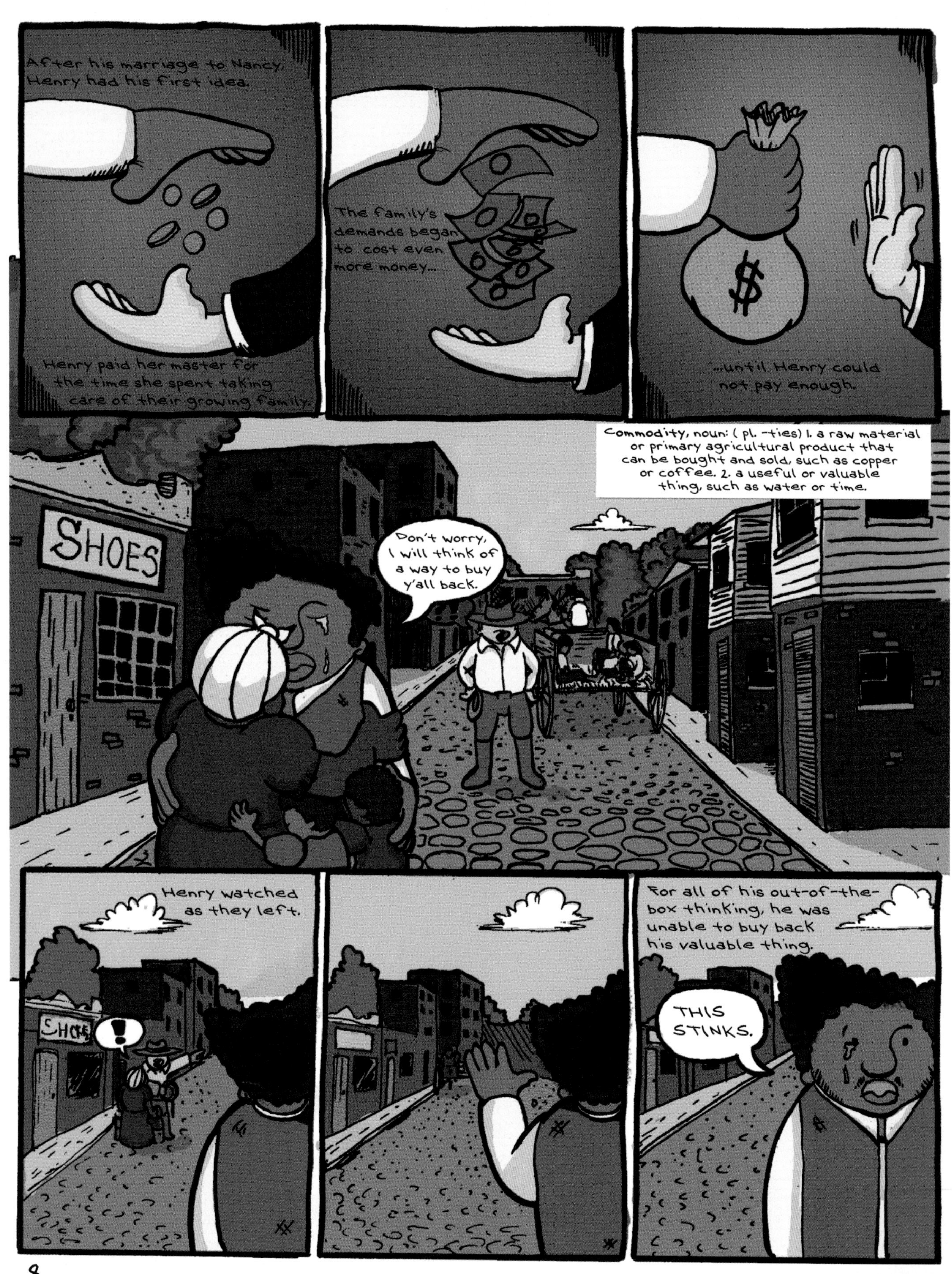

After his marriage to Nancy, Henry had his first idea.
Henry paid her master for the time she spent taking care of their growing family.
The family's demands began to cost even more money...
$
...until Henry could not pay enough.
Commodity, noun: (pl. -ties) 1. a raw material or primary agricultural product that can be bought and sold, such as copper or coffee. 2. a useful or valuable thing, such as water or time.
SHOES
Don't worry, I will think of a way to buy y'all back.
Henry watched as they left.
!
For all of his out-of-the-box thinking, he was unable to buy back his valuable thing.
THIS STINKS.

Following the loss of his family, Henry found life extremely difficult. He spent days trying to think of some way to get his wife and children back.

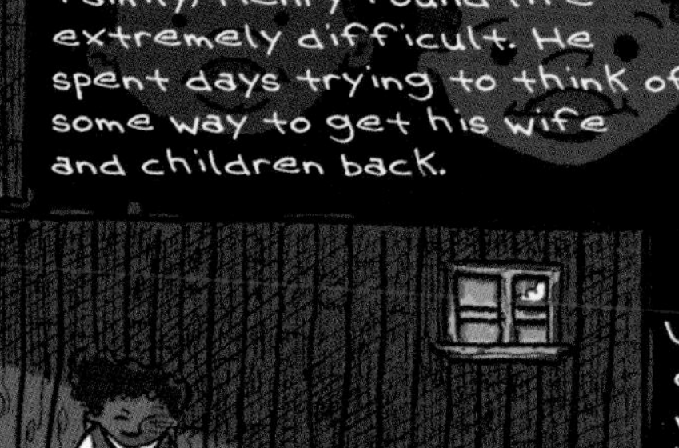

Uncertainty was the worst part of being a slave. The things that made the definition of liberty so important to the Founding Fathers were mere trivialities to slave owners.

Henry spent weeks lost in the "trivial," until...

GET TO WORK, BOY!

Monotony, noun: the monotony of everyday life, tedium, tediousness, lack of variety, dullness, boredom, repetitiveness, uniformity, routineness, tiresomeness, lack of excitement, uneventfulness, dreariness, colorlessness, featurelessness, informal deadliness.

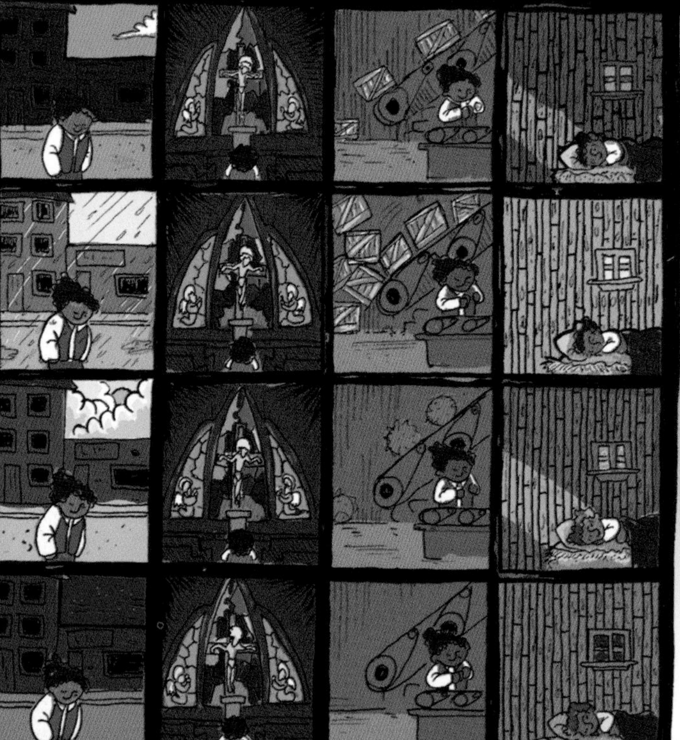

THIS STINKS!!
HENRY, IT IS TIME FOR YOU TO LEAVE. GO BUY SOME SHOES.

God spoke to Henry and gave him a plan.

Good mornin', Henry. How are you?
The Lord, umm...told me, uhh...to buy some shoes.
The shopkeeper was a good man.
I umm... think he uhhh... wants me to umm... umm...uhhhh... run away.
But he was also white, and Henry was still a slave.
Henry, I have good shoes, so I can help you with that, and I have friends in Philadelphia, so I think I can help you, umm... run away.
Abolitionist, noun: a person who favors the abolition of a practice or institution, esp. slavery.
NORTH
NORTH
NORTH
Henry would need a considerable amount of money for the plan to work.
But slaves knew how to work hard.
For Henry, this was all in a day's work.

After months of planning, the shopkeeper and his abolitionist cohorts waited for Henry.
He should be here very soon.
I pray he has not been delayed.
To say that Henry was in a hurry would be an understatement.
RIIINNNGGGGG
GOOD LORD!!!
Irony: often mistakenly used in place of coincidence.
SHOES
THIS STINKS.
LANCA
SHIP HIGH IN TRANSIT
OVER WARE
For a while things went smoothly,
SHIP HIGH IN TRANS
PHILADEL PENNSI
as Henry traveled by different means.
THIS END UP
However, it became more trying.

UPSIDE DOWN WASN'T SO BAD.

NEITHER WAS THE CRAMPED SPACE,

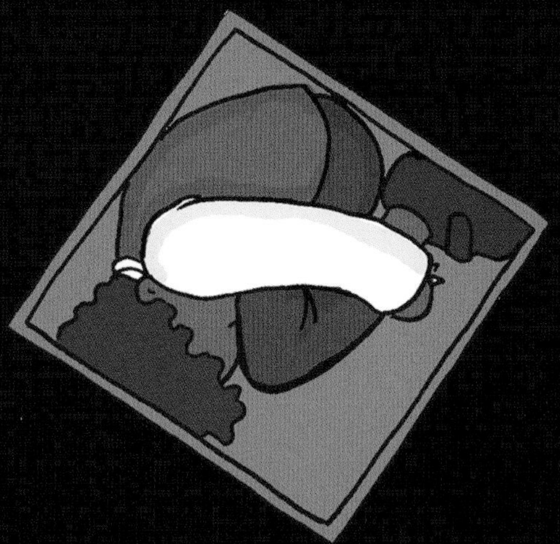

OR 27 HOURS.

ALONE IN THE DARK
WAS NOT NEARLY AS BAD...

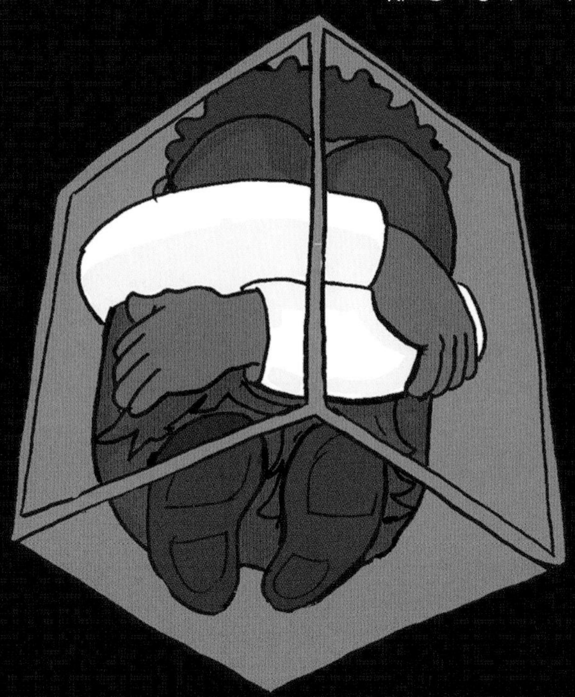

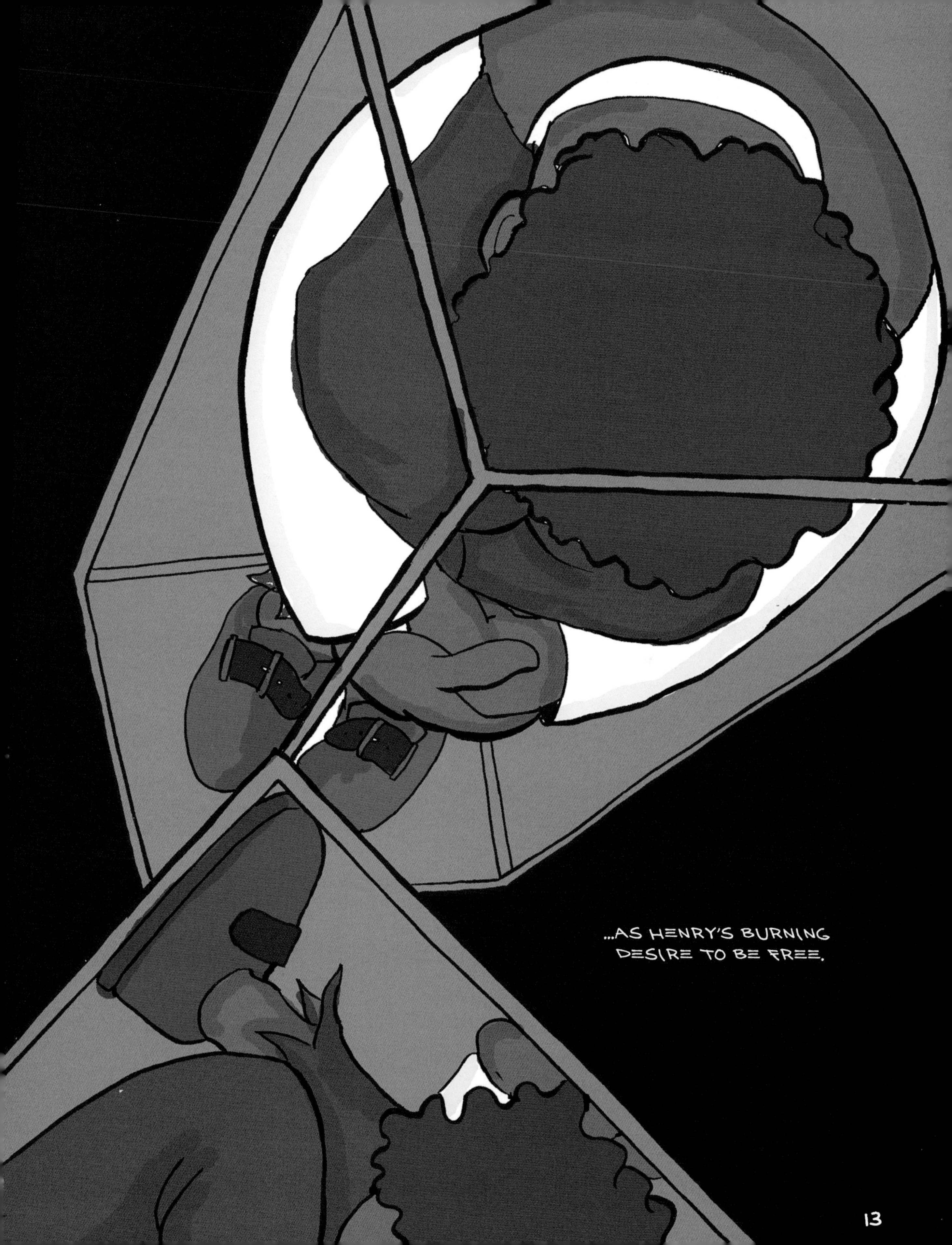
...AS HENRY'S BURNING
DESIRE TO BE FREE.

There was great anticipation when he finally arrived.
All right then, sir?
Very well. Thank you Kindly.
According to written accounts and a lithograph by Samuel Rowse, this is how the scene appeared. Henry's dramatic escape ended when he sang a prearranged hymn. However, realistically it was probably more like...
All right then, sir?
LET ME OUT!!!
Gotta pee!!!

Henry's life became his own.
Soon after his escape, he made it better.
Then he began to rebuild, but soon his life took a turn.
Abalish!
End it.
Henry gave speech after...
...speech until the Fugitive Slave Act of 1850.
Henry had no choice so...

History lost track of Henry and his family soon thereafter. There are accounts in his book, Mirror, about the horrors of slavery and his traveling show where he became a magician. Ultimately, Henry lived the rest of his life quite unlike the beginning...

...Out of the Box.

END

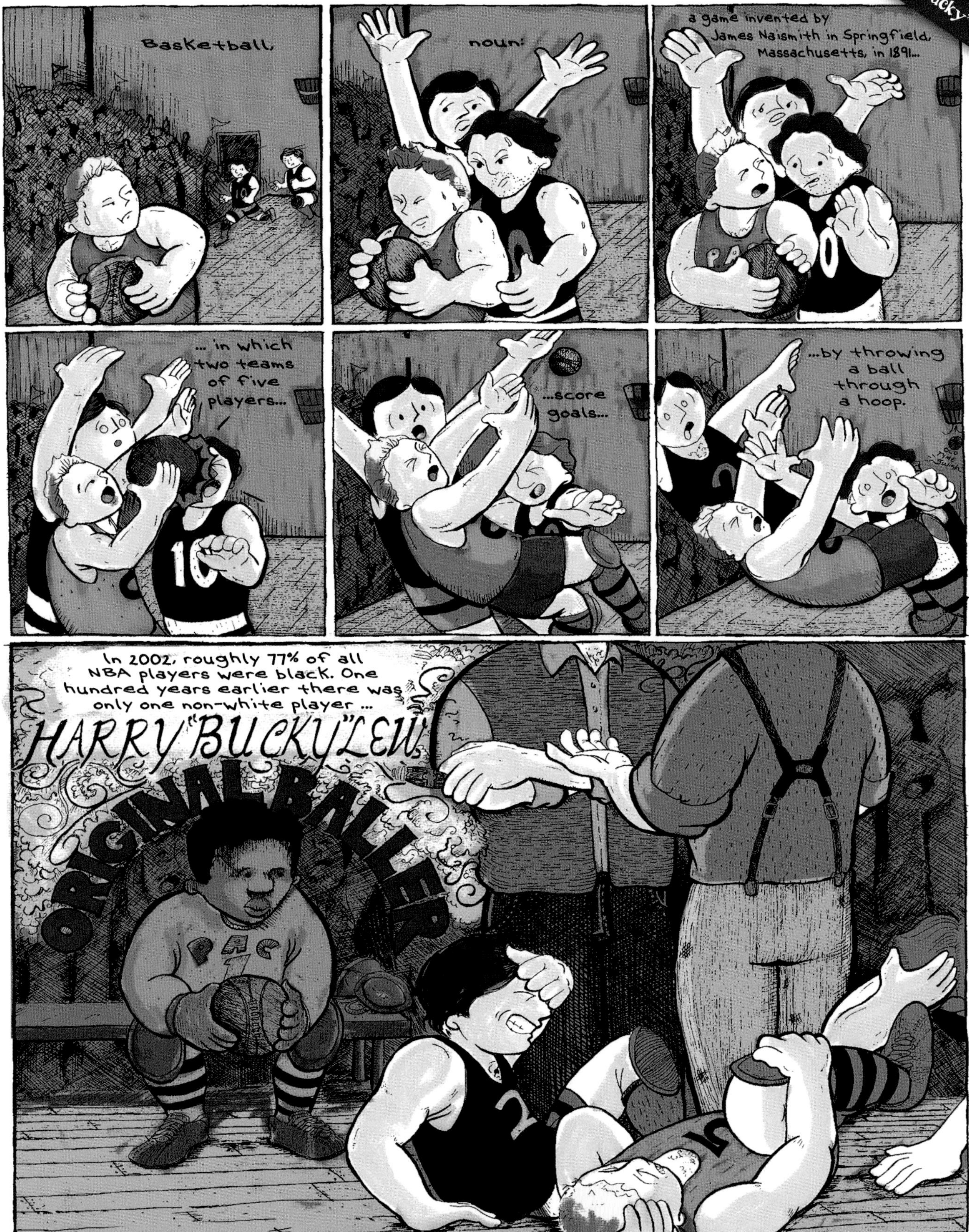

In 2002, roughly 77% of all NBA players were black. One hundred years earlier there was only one non-white player ...

HARRY "BUCKY" LEW,

ORIGINAL BALLER

Harry's pedigree
Barzillai Lew
Fifer for Captain John Ford's 27th Regiment, Chelmsford, MA
Harry's great-grandfather
Harry's grandparents
Adrastus and Elizabeth Lew
Conductors on the Underground Railroad
RUNAWAY
SLAVE
Harry's uncle
ZADOCK LEW
owned one of the largest libraries in New England
THE LEW FAMILY of MASSACHUSETTS
BOUND by MUSIC
Peter Lew
Grand Master Freemason
Harry's great-uncle
Harry Lew was born into a trailblazing free black educated family in Massachusetts.
The Lews were important and were also known all over New England for their musical prowess.
William Lew
Equal rights activist and business owner
Harry's father
So, it was no surprise that Harry was a gifted student and athlete. In addition, he was a talented musician, like all those Lews who had come before.

After graduating high school, Harry joined the local youth basketball team in Lowell, Massachusetts.

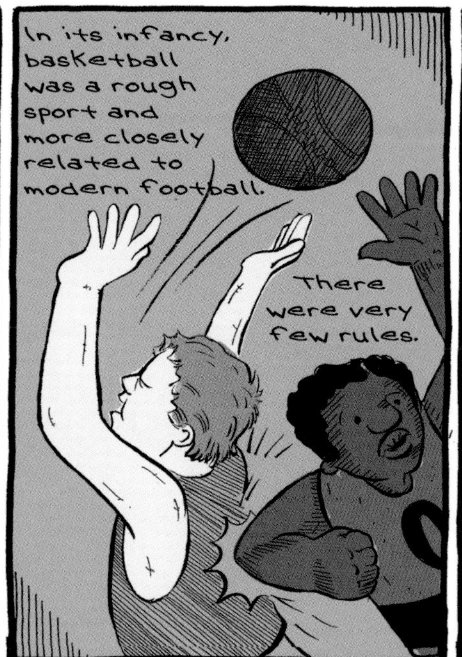
In its infancy, basketball was a rough sport and more closely related to modern football.
There were very few rules.

Despite the tough conditions (or maybe because of them), Harry proved to be a dominant defensive player.
So for the next four years, he showed just how dominant he could be.
Way to go, Bucky! Pass it over here!

98
CHAMPS

99

00

01

With none of the fanfare that accompanies modern signing, Harry became a guard with the
PAWTUCKETVILLE ATHLETIC CLUB.
Contract

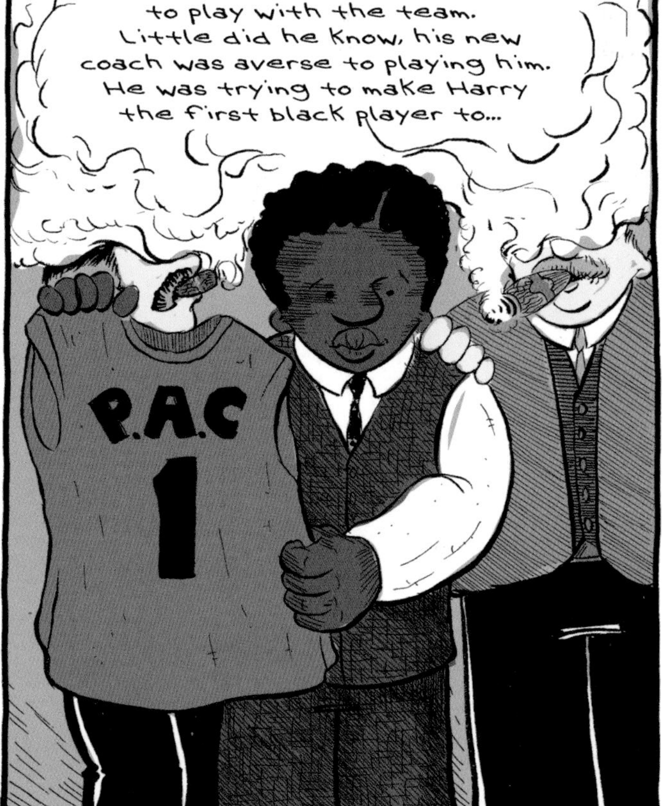
Harry was paid $5.00 a day to play with the team. Little did he know, his new coach was averse to playing him. He was trying to make Harry the first black player to...
P.A.C
1

The New England Professional Basketball League soon folded. However, Harry "Bucky" Lew went on to play with other teams. Some teams that he put together himself went barnstorming all over New England. He played in events all over until he was 42.

Is it a coincidence that Brown drafted both the first black NBA player - Chuck Cooper - and one of the first black NBA superstars, Bill Russell? All of this just a few miles from where Bucky Lew made history as the Original Baller?
END

Trick, noun:
a skillful act performed for entertainment or amusement.

Illusion, noun: false idea or belief.
Nothing up my sleeve.

Richard Potter's GREATEST ILLUSION

Richard Potter was the first American stage magician. The Indian rope trick was one of his most famous stunts.

However, it was not his greatest illusion.

Goodness!

Devil's work!

Where did he go?

That is amazing!

That is just amazing.

Did you see that?

Is it witchcraft?

How in the world did he do it?

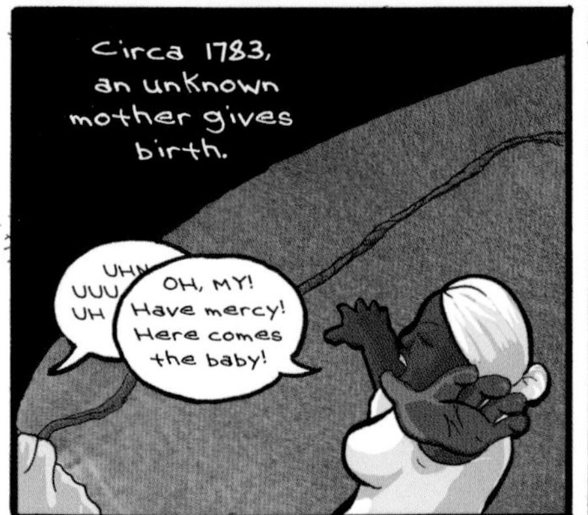

Circa 1783, an unknown mother gives birth.
OH, MY! Have mercy! Here comes the baby!

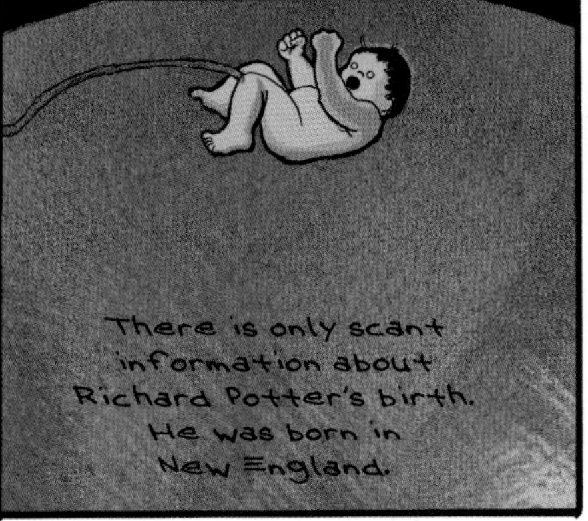

There is only scant information about Richard Potter's birth. He was born in New England.

Circa 1783, an English baronet has a son.

Richard was a smart boy.

The baronet did his best to educate Richard.

Time for you to travel!

So Richard spent some time traveling.

Atlantic Ocean

North Sea

Sweden

Russia

Bay of Biscay

French Empire

Black Sea

Spain

Mediterranean Sea

Africa

...my next trick...
One day, Potter came upon a curious crowd.

Levitation!

Excuse me!

From that moment on, Potter was captivated by prestidigitation.

After years of study, Potter came home with a plan in mind.

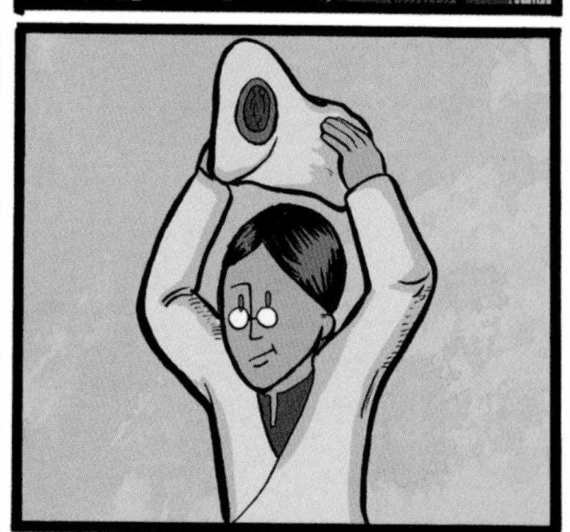

Shortly thereafter, Potter began his career.

Greetings and salutations. Gather 'round, friends, as I seek to amuse and amaze you with feats of conjuring and prestidigitation that will no doubt thrill and entertain!

Potter began to perform his shows.
His reputation as a showman increased.
TAXES
RUNAW
HENRY
M. POTTER MAGICIAN

As Potter's reputation grew...
WANTED
REWARD
M. POTTER

...so did his popularity.
While honing his skills, he began to perform all manner of tricks.
THE FAMOUS MR POTTER

I believe this to be your card.

Oh, my! Only moments ago, it was but a small thing!

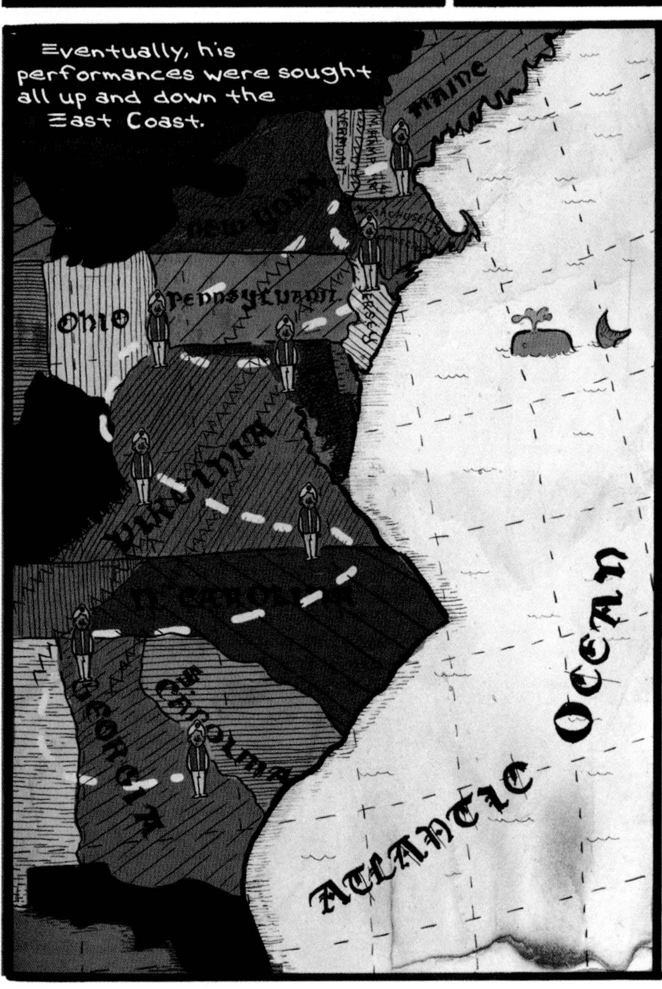
Eventually, his performances were sought all up and down the East Coast.
MAINE
VERMONT
NEW YORK
OHIO
PENNSYLVANIA
VIRGINIA
ATLANTIC OCEAN

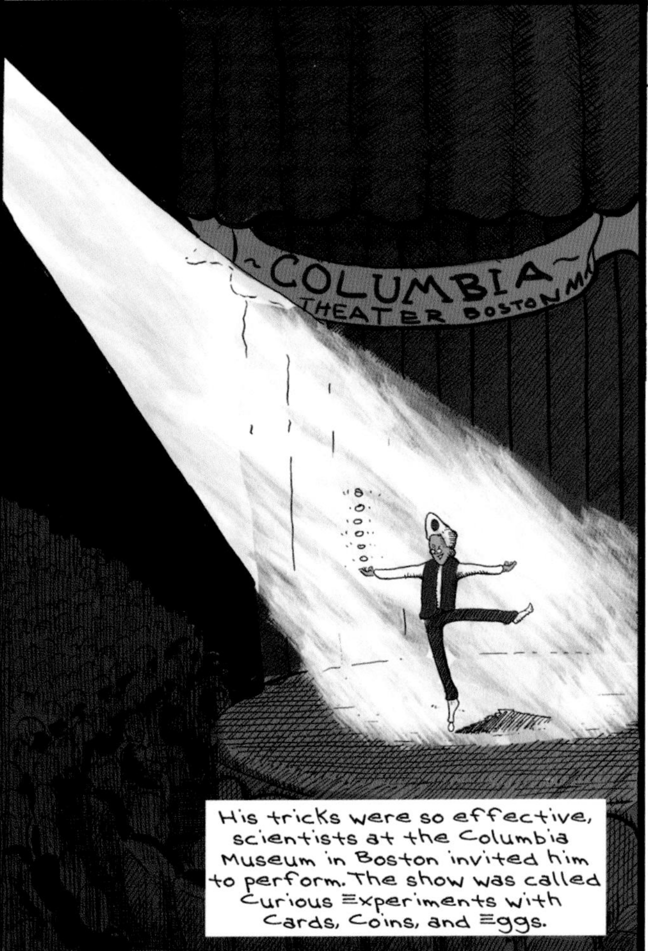
COLUMBIA
THEATER BOSTON

His tricks were so effective, scientists at the Columbia Museum in Boston invited him to perform. The show was called Curious Experiments with Cards, Coins, and Eggs.

Potter became an expert in all the tricks of his trade.

I AM A POOR POOR BIRD IN A BIG BLACK POT HOW, oh how I wish to Fly free!

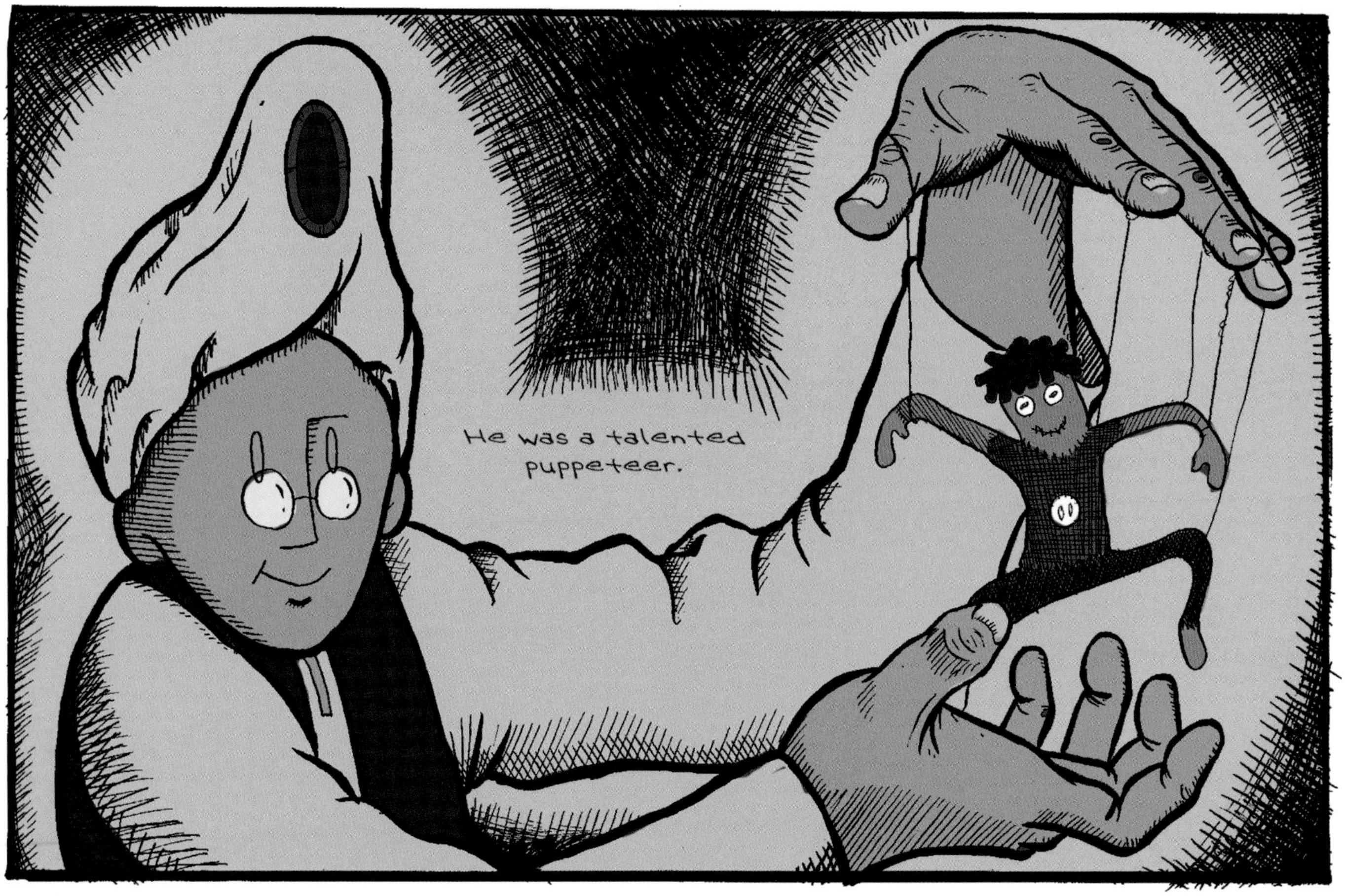

He was a talented puppeteer.

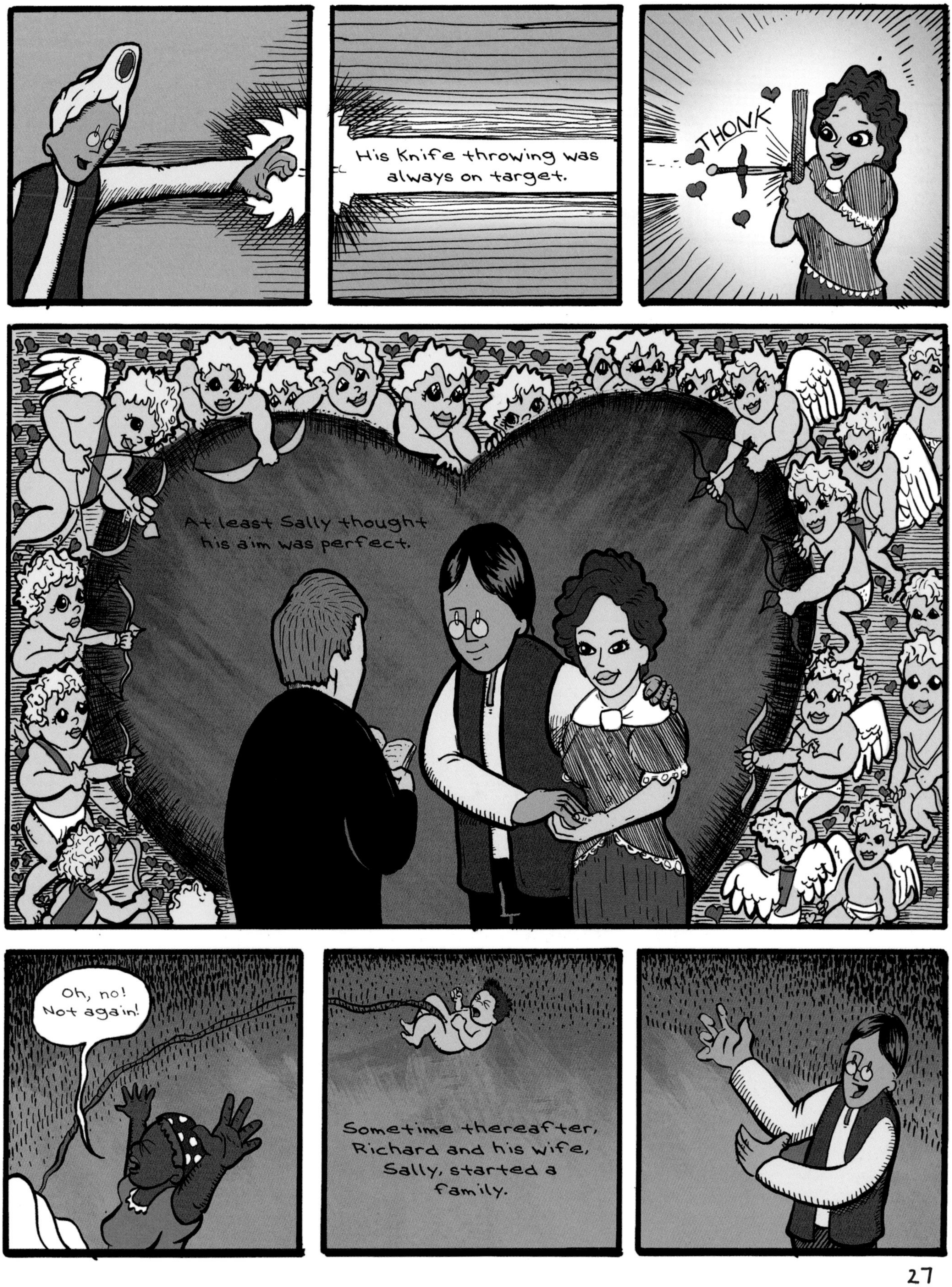

His knife throwing was always on target.

THONK

At least Sally thought his aim was perfect.

Oh, no! Not again!

Sometime thereafter, Richard and his wife, Sally, started a family.

Magicians are performers that thrive o
reputation. Building their reputation he
create demand for their shows. The
greater the demand, the greater the
per performance. Sometimes the rumor
their feats are greatly exaggerate
often than not, they have adm
things that did not happe
some of the legends tha
Potter traveled and

ore
ed to
Here are
emerged as
rformed.

On one occasion, Potter happened upon some farmers.

They were at their wits' end, but Potter had a trick up his sleeve.

CLUCK?

Potter attached the chicken to the cart.
Dang it!

THEN
SNAP

Magically, in a few seconds the chicken was able to do what the ox would not.

WHEW!

Afterward, the cart resumed its previous position.

?

On another occasion his travels took him to a local tavern.

The locals were less than excited to have him.

YOUR NEEDLESS INHOSPITABLE BEHAVIOR HAS OFFENDED THE SPIRITS OF THE ETHER

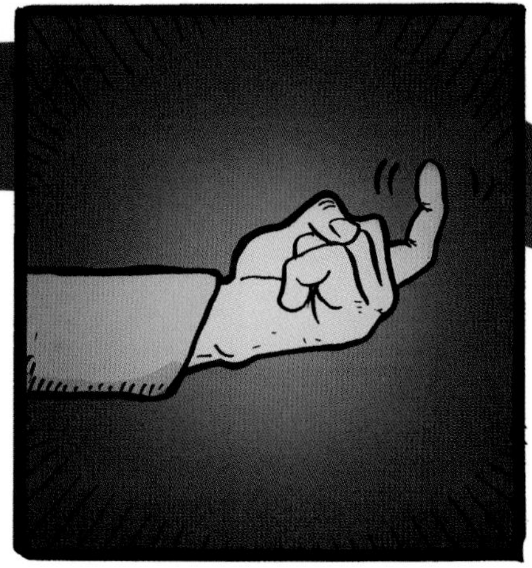

As you can see, this stove is a roaring furnace.

This, dear friends, is an uncooked ham.

I will place it here to cook for a while.

I will now climb into the stove to see just how the ham is cooking. Do not worry, friends, the ham will be fine.

Presto, I have been in the furnace not unlike that of a fiery volcano, and I have returned with the ham, ready to eat.
CLAP
CLAP
CLAP
CLAP
CLAP
CLAP

Eventually, Potter became very wealthy, commanding $5,000 for a 20-day engagement. Soon, he was able to purchase an estate in New Hampshire.

SOLD
Welcome home.

For the rest of his days, Potter, Sally, and their children lived in luxury. He threw extravagant dinner parties with lots of well-to-do friends.

Welcome to my home. Eat and enjoy!

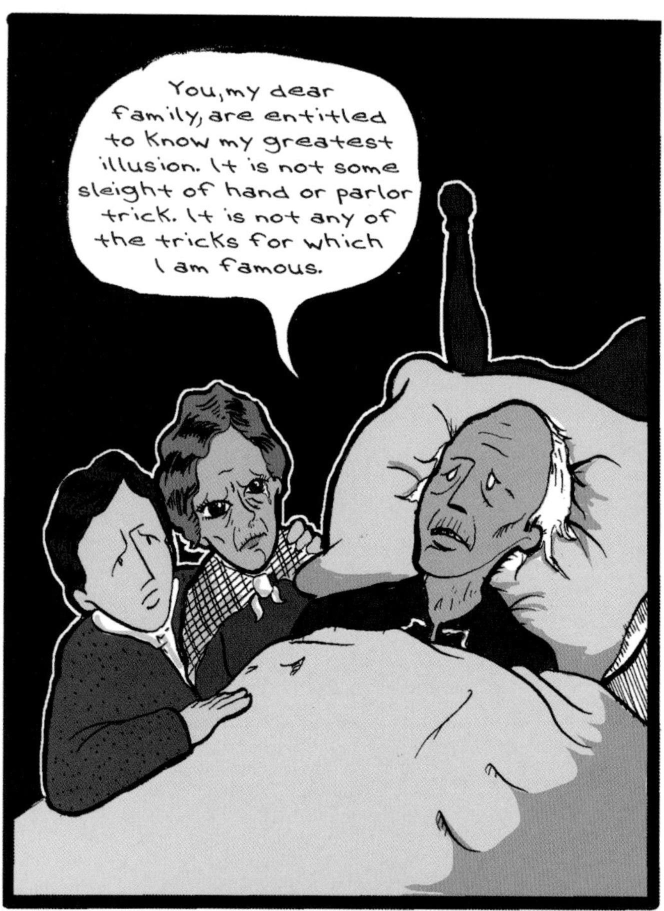
You, my dear family, are entitled to know my greatest illusion. It is not some sleight of hand or parlor trick. It is not any of the tricks for which I am famous.

The world has known the great illusionist Richard Potter as an Indian from the far-flung exotic Orient.

"My mother was a black serving woman. She was my father's slave."

"My greatest illusion is that I am and have always been a black man."

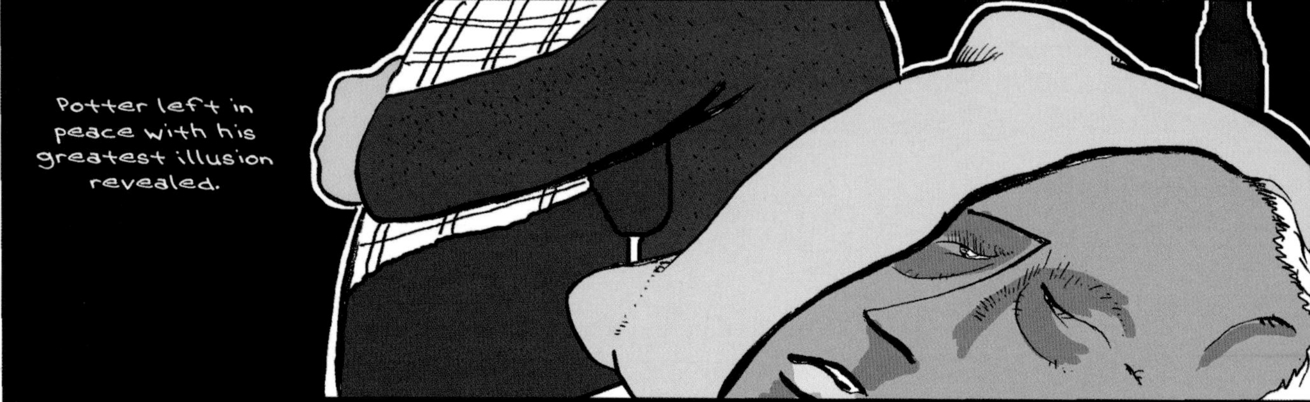
Potter left in peace with his greatest illusion revealed.

In Memory of
RICHARD POTTER
The Celebrated VENTRILOQUIST
Who died Sept. 20, 1835
Aged 52 years
In Memory of
SALLY H.
Wife of
RICHARD POTTER
Who died
Oct. 24, 1836
Potter Place, New Hampshire, is where Richard and his wife now rest. He lives on in the history of magic as the first American stage magician. Potter is forever free from all magic and illusion. However, his memory lives on because of his greatest illusion.
END

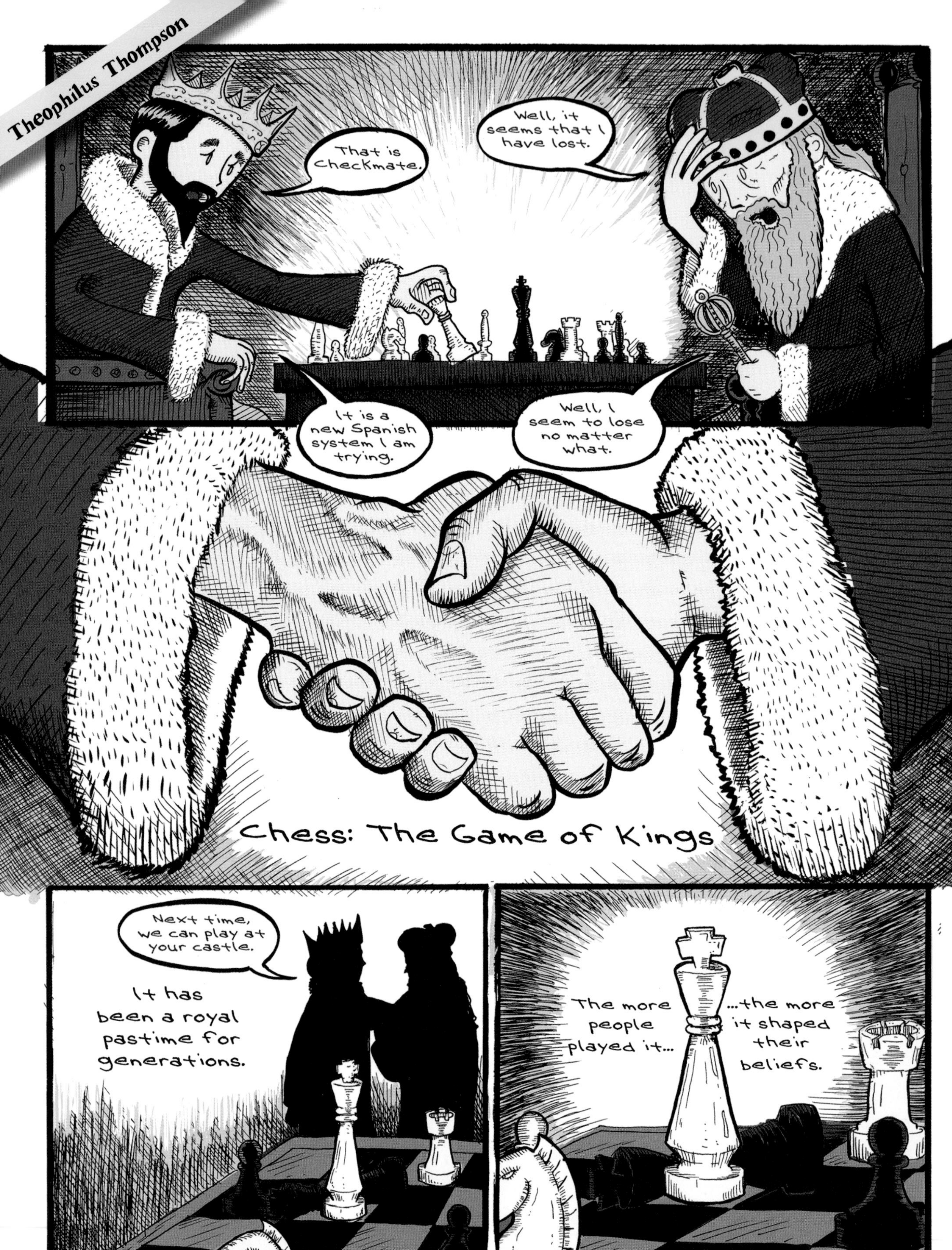
Theophilus Thompson
That is Checkmate.
Well, it seems that I have lost.
It is a new Spanish system I am trying.
Well, I seem to lose no matter what.
Chess: The Game of Kings
Next time, we can play at your castle.
It has been a royal pastime for generations.
The more people played it...
...the more it shaped their beliefs.

In the beginning, the metaphor for a kingdom was a king's body.
The army of the kingdom was interpreted as his arm, and so on.
Then in the Middle Ages, chess became popular.
So much so that people became obsessed with chess.
So the metaphor changes to chess.
Every person has a place, and moves independently of the king. They all play on the board and go back in the same bag in the end.

So, if one were to take the metaphor to its logical end, then the white pawn is a peasant — a peasant that can advance first and has a built-in advantage just by being white.
This means that the black piece has a built-in second-class status. It goes second, and that disadvantage makes the difference, which makes this story of a pawn-to-King promotion all the more impressive. Here is the story of...
Theophilus Thompson

Theophilus Thompson was a slave born in 1855 in Frederick, Maryland.

As a child, Thompson witnessed the war that ended the horrible practice.

After the war, he spent time working in a number of jobs available to former slaves.

Thompson later found himself working for a man named John Hanshew.
Checkmate!
Thompson noticed Hanshew and a friend playing a peculiar game.
Good game!

I see you have discovered my passion.

Sorry, sir... I uh -

These make the game easier to learn.

Determination, noun: a resolute movement toward some object or end.

The next day, he showed his employer what he had learned.

I believe that is checkmate.
Indeed.

I think you might do well in a tournament.

CHICAGO
For a novice he did well.
Thompson won some.
Draw!
And he lost some.
He won some really good ones too.
By the end he had gained some admirers.
1. KP3
2. QP3
3. P-KN3
4 B-KN2
5. KP4
6. N-KB3
7 N-QB3
8. O-O
9. Q-Q2
11. Q4
12 K4
KP3
N-KBP3
Q3
QB-B4
KB-Q2
N-QR2
Q4
B-Q4
R-N1
O-O-O
Q5
He used his newfound attention to write a book: Chess Problems: Either to Play and Mate.

Thompson was well on his way to becoming a national chess star.
His book was successful, and he was playing great in correspondence games.
Then he vanished.
There were lots of theories as to his whereabouts.
Some were far more sinister than others.
No matter what his fate, Theophilus Thompson left his imprint on the game of chess.
Thompson went from being a slave to the first recognized black chess master. With that accomplishment he proved that while it might be more difficult, it is possible to win with the black pieces.
END

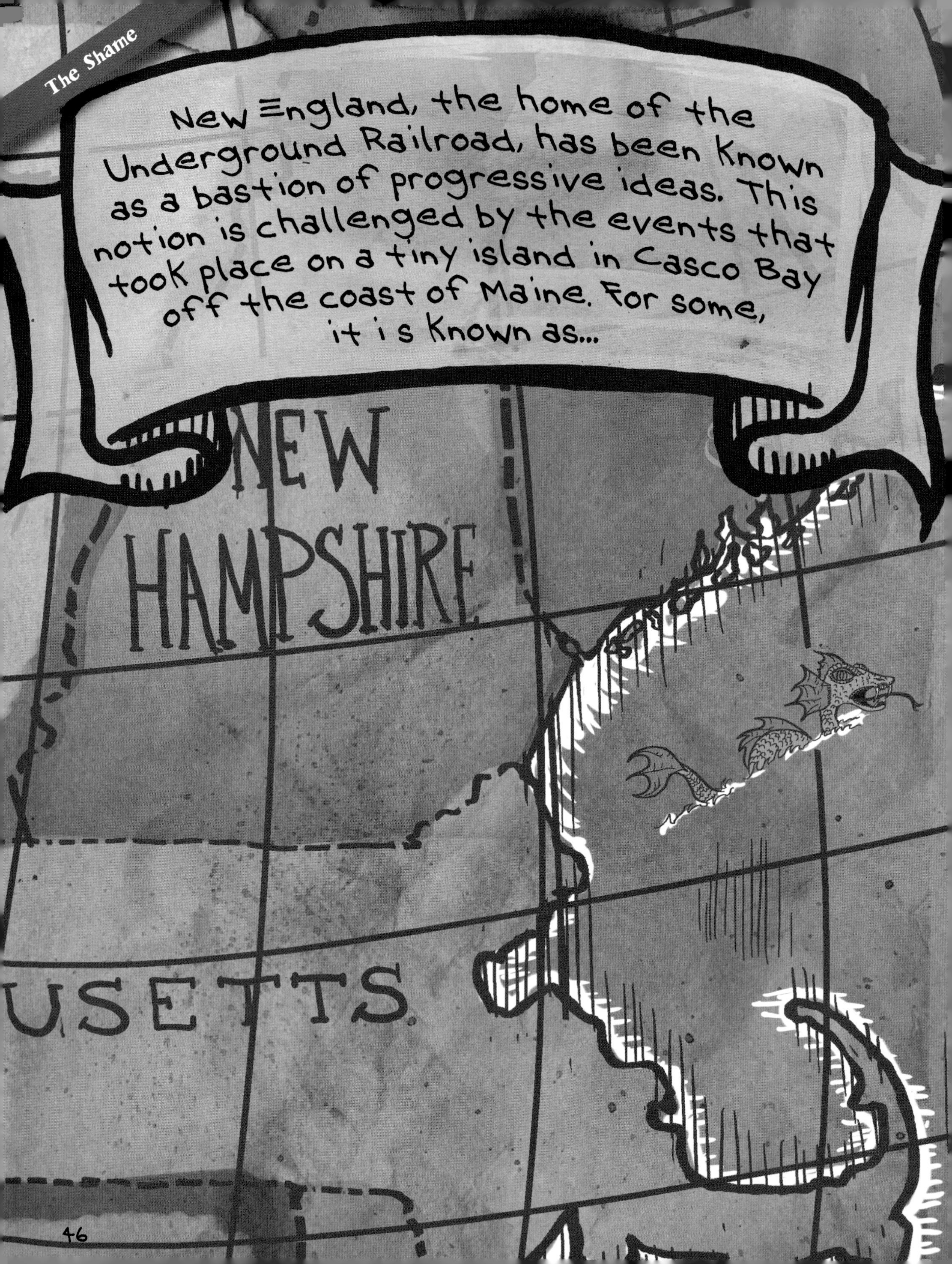

New England, the home of the Underground Railroad, has been known as a bastion of progressive ideas. This notion is challenged by the events that took place on a tiny island in Casco Bay off the coast of Maine. For some, it is known as...

NEW HAMPSHIRE

USETTS

The Shame

It all starts here in Casco Bay. Off the coast of Maine there is a quiet place that is now known as Vacationland.

The Maine coastal communities have a lot to offer potential vacationers. It is the perfect destination for Bostonians looking for a quick getaway or rich southerners searching for a cool climate.

One hundred fifty years ago it was just an island.

And this was just a day...

...until a storm changed everything.

THUNDER

THUNDER
You alright, Master?

You saved my life when you did not have to. You could've let me die.

THUNDER
You needed saving, sir. I did the right thing.

Captain Darling
His slave, Benjamin
He rewarded Ben's heroic act with money and his freedom.

With his newfound freedom and wealth, Benjamin Darling bought an island and became the founding father of the Malaga Island community.

This looks like a good place to start.

Benjamin Darling
Founder
Benjamin Darling's family lived on the island after he died. Later, they were joined by others.
The new arrivals married Darling's descendants and soon the island was full.

It was not an extravagant life, but it was a life nonetheless.

And in the summertime they would have great views.

However, others soon noticed the Malaga inhabitants' lifestyle... and views.
We have to do something about those living conditions.
Ye$. We do. Did you see the view$?

Some felt that it was their Christian duty to save the people on Malaga Island. So some women from the Women's Christian Temperance Union visited Malaga.

Welcome!

During their tour, they saw people living their lives.

Unfortunately, the women saw from their own perspectives.

Using some of their contacts, they petitioned the governor for help.

Governor Frederick W. Plaisted wanted to see for himself.

However, his perspective was just as skewed.
You were right. This is horrible.

These people should enjoy the same rights that all Mainers have. They need new homes and clean water.
Politicians are known to say one thing and do another. Plaisted was no different. While he spoke publicly about the rights of Malagites, a fight was raging over responsibility for the islanders.
Harpswell did not want them.
Shiftless
Miscegenation
Criminals
Monsters
Runaway Slaves
Eugenics
Phippsburg did not want them.
Inbred
Eyesore
Mongrels
Immoral
Half-breeds
Blight
Half-wit
The newspapers wrote about the Malagites, and there were vicious editorials.
Rumor and innuendo turned these regular people into subhuman monsters.

According to a theory in the radio documentary *Malaga Island: A Story Best Left Untold* by Rob Rosenthal and Kate Philbrick, interests were about to collide.

The Women's Christian Temperance Union was in league with the governor as champions of the Malagites. However, they disapproved of his other endeavors.

XXX

BALLOT
YES
NO

NO
YES

NO
YES

By order of the state of Maine you are hereby evicted. Vacate the island, NOW!
LCOME!

For the islanders this was an amazing turn of events. Almost overnight they went from having a modest home to being homeless.

Most of the islanders saw the writing on the wall and left the island right away. Others were not so lucky.
Could you please use this telephone?
What is a tell-e-fone?
I see...
After the remaining islanders were tested under dubious circumstances, they were committed.
MAINE SCHOOL FOR THE FEEBLE MINDED

All of the remaining buildings and anything left behind were burned to the ground.

Then they dug up the graves.

The state combined the remains of the 17 deceased Malagites into 5 coffins.

Of the 50 or so remaining men, women, and children, 1/5 were committed and castrated.

To add insult to injury the state also committed the dead to the School for Feeble Minded.

Some tried to remain...

...in spite of the hostility.

Some turned to the church for support.
Surely they'll help.

No we won't!

In an odd coincidence, some of the Malagites migrated south to find a better life. This was an oddity in a time when most people of color migrated north.

There were some who could "pass." This meant that they could pass as a white person.

However, at times their past would still haunt them.
RONG COLOR EYES
PRONOUNCED BROW
SUSPICIOUS SKIN
WIDE

After some time passed, they were able to live in relative peace as long as their past was hidden.

No one has lived on the island since the eviction. Most people know of the incident because of Rob Rosenthal and Kate Philbrick's documentary and an exhibition at The Maine State Museum.

Not much has changed since 1911. Governor John Baldacci issued a formal apology in 2010 to the descendants of the island's inhabitants. Now the only thing left is a scarred memory, an empty island, and incredible views.
END

KNOCK
KNOCK

Hello, Father. I wonder if I can ask you a few questions?

Come in, son. Have a seat.

Thank you, sir.

So, what can I do for you this afternoon?

I have some questions about equality in the American education system. I wonder if you can tell me of your experience. I have heard a remarkable story about an integrated school. I forget the name...
Oh, so you want to hear about my time in New Hampshire at...

The NOYES Academy

Well, I was born in 1819, and was raised in New York in a remarkable community of free negro people called the Free Africans. My father, Boston, was freed as an adult, and my mother, Charity, was born free. My parents were God-fearing abolitionist people, and they raised me as such. Even as a child I wanted to be a minister. At first I was educated by private tutors and at a few other schools in and around New York. After I graduated, I continued my quest to become a true man of God. That was when I heard of an amazing school in the free state of New Hampshire: The Noyes Academy. This was well before emancipation and freedom for the millions of slaves in America. Nevertheless, I began the arduous journey to northern NH. This turned out to be much harder than I would have imagined.

PLATFORM 9 3/4

It was a long journey, so I figured I would go by train. Even though this was years before Jim Crow...

...he found a way to hinder my every move.
CAW

CAW!

Some people took pity on me,
even as others objected.

Thanks for the ri-

Finally, my journey was complete, and this place was a sight to behold.

I was in Canaan, New Hampshire, and far from the savagery of slavery. Noyes would help me in my journey to become a man of God.

My excitement could not belie my apprehension. I had a troubling, long journey, and I was still a free black man among white people.

My fears were unfounded.
!

Friends, help me to extend a warm welcome to Alexander Crummell!

These people treated me like no other white people had ever treated me...

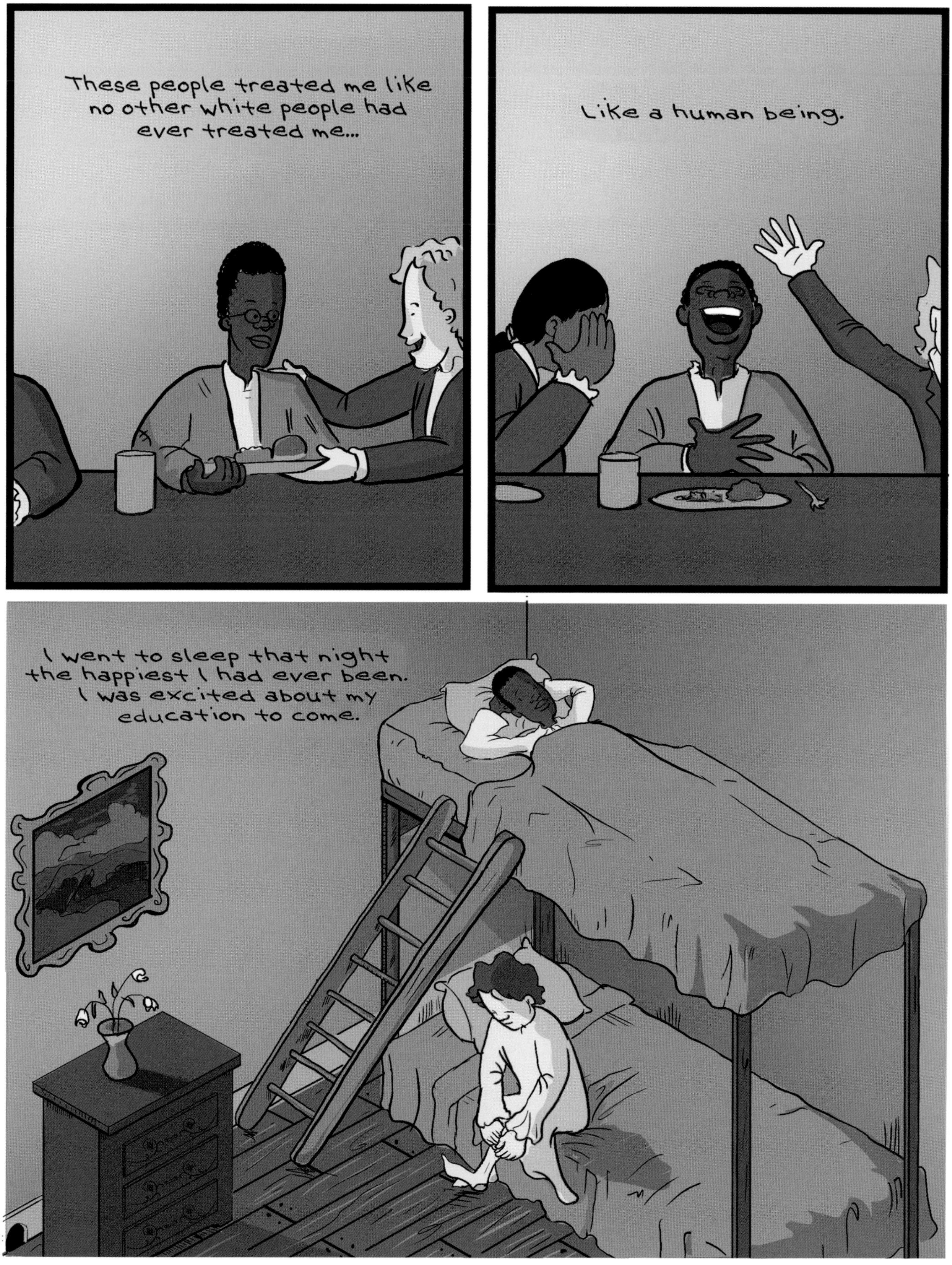

Like a human being.

I went to sleep that night the happiest I had ever been. I was excited about my education to come.

C
B
A
$a^2+b^2=c^2$
[a,b]

The school was all I could have hoped for. They took us through a rigorous course of study. We were instructed in science, mathematics, history, and philosophy. The courses were hard and I spent many a night working into the wee hours, writing papers by candlelight. The professors were knowledgeable people and good instructors. They were stern but fair.

Yet, I did not realize, and could never have imagined, the storm that was brewing over our very presence in Canaan. I did not see him, but old Jim Crow had crept his way into New England and was about to destroy this glorious place.

All the towns in the vicinity took a vote, and they decided that our little school had to go.
Order!

They gathered at our door
with murderous intent.

Racism and bigotry had infected the townspeople. They were determined to remove the entire school — with us inside.

We had no choice. We had to fight back.
POW

POW
POW
The shots were not fired at the mob. The shots were fired to create some time for us to escape.

After we were gone, they dragged the house to a nearby swamp.
CAW!

I watched as the school disappeared.

The Noyes Academy was gone.

I eventually finished my education.

Racism dogged my every move...
...but it could not hold me back.

It was a beautiful dream. Alas, America was not ready at the time.

Maybe someday...

Well, thank you for your time, sir.
Anytime. By the way, what's your name?

My name is William, but I am Known as W.E.B. DuBois.

END

Marshall "Major" Taylor
Bicycle racing, or cycling, was the most popular sport in America in the late 19th and early 20th centuries.
It is extremely competitive.
In the late 1890s, it was even harder if you were black. Back then you had to be the fastest because that was the only way to outrun Jim Crow. Defeating him was a colossal undertaking.

It was and is a physically taxing sport.
To be successful, it takes skill and mental toughness.
One man was fast enough.

Marshall "Major" Taylor

The Blac

CYCLONE

Marshall Taylor was born to Gilbert and Saphronia in Louisville, Kentucky.
Boy, that was fast!
Taylor was fast from the start.

He was born into a large family, and being one of many it was hard to get noticed.
His hand

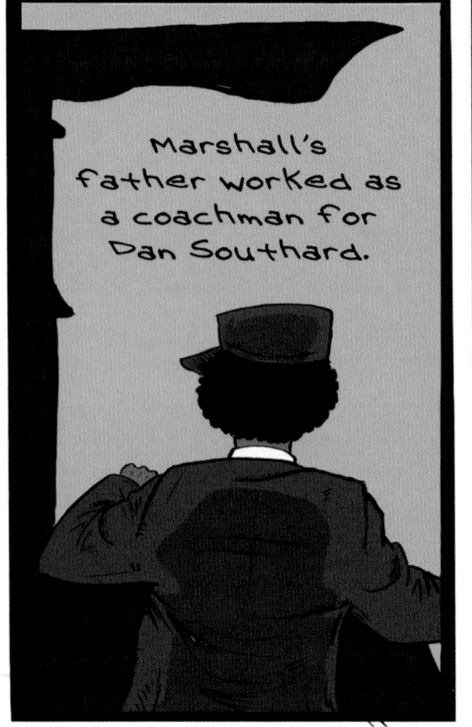
Marshall's father worked as a coachman for Dan Southard.

Mornin', Mr. Danny.
Hi, Mr. Gilbert.

Mr. Southard, mind if we make a quick stop this mornin'?
That should be fine, Gilbert. We are in no hurry today.

Gilbert loved and cared for his children. However, his time was limited with each because he had so many.
Hey, Kid!
So, Marshall spent a lot of his time alone.
My name's Danny.
It is time to go, boys.
I'm Marshall.
Gilbert, why don't you bring him along? He can keep Danny company.

The boys got along so well that the Southards invited him to stay the night.

Who can tell me the capital of Peru?
He eventually came to stay all the time and was educated alongside Danny.

Hey, boys, I have a surprise for you.
They treated him like family.

Brand-new Bicycles!
By all measures he was family.

The gift of the bicycle was a greater gift than the Southards could have known.
Hey! Wait up! You are so much faster than I am!

When the Southards had to leave they wanted to take Marshall with them.
Sorry. I can't go.

The best friend Marshall had ever known left.

Marshall would carry on.

He carried on so well he started to attract attention.

You are a talented young man.
Thanks.

Are you interested in working for me?
Doing what?

You can do bicycle tricks outside my store.

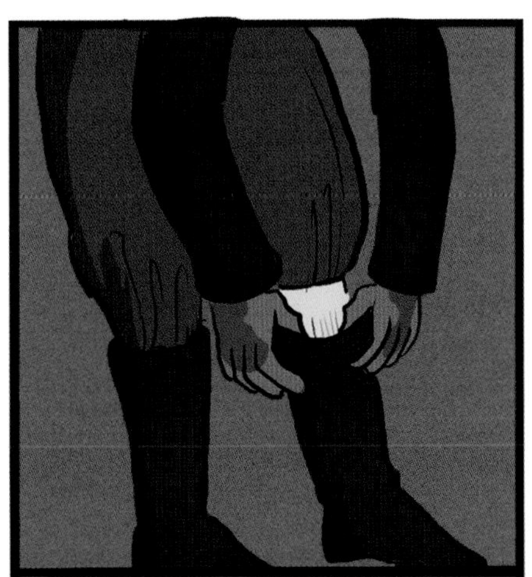

He adopted a character and began to perform as Major Taylor.

Gather 'round as I perform death-defying feats of agility and skill, while balancing on two wheels!

Marshall was content with his life, until one day...

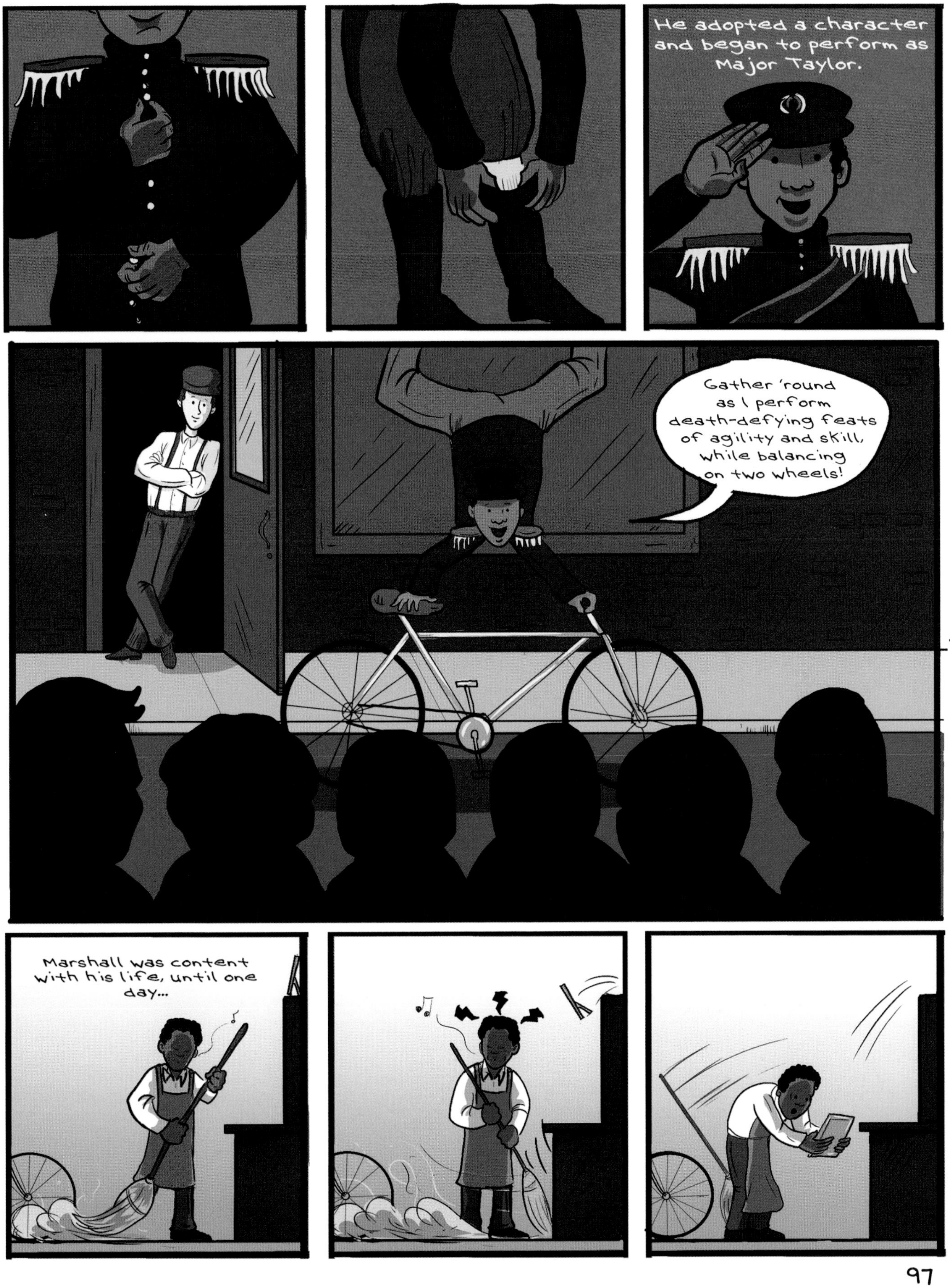

...he found something that
would forever change it.
CYCLING

Marshall entered his first race
with the support of his employer.
Ready!
Set...

Not only was he
talented, he
was fast.
...GO!
DUST

Ready! Set...
Marshall began to train with his employer.

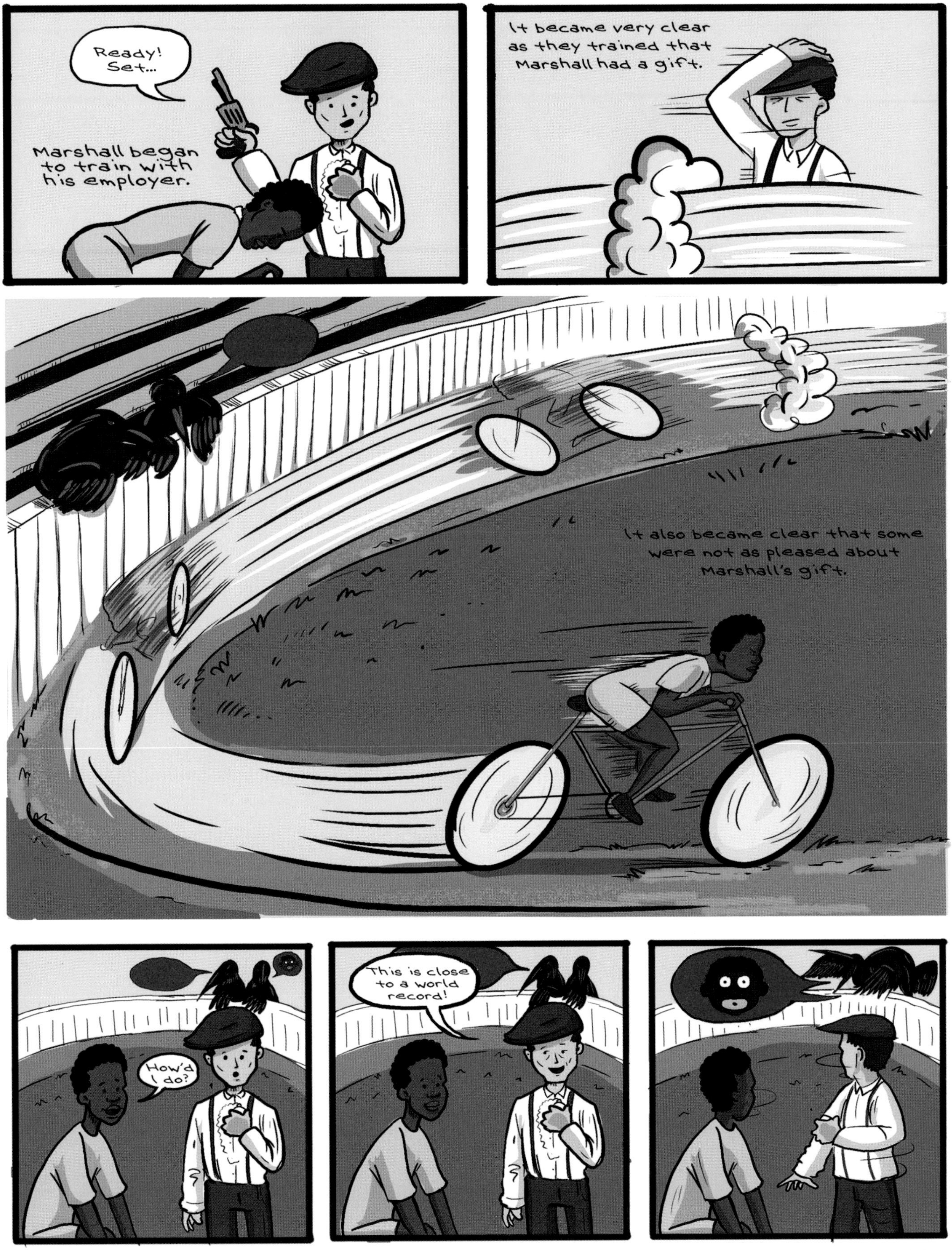

It became very clear as they trained that Marshall had a gift.

It also became clear that some were not as pleased about Marshall's gift.

How'd I do?

This is close to a world record!

DING
DING
DING
Welcome!
The next day it was worse.

I think you boys should leave. NOW!

You know, you're ready for bigger things.

So, with the help of his employer, Marshall left for a job in Massachusetts, where he would train and race professionally.

WORCESTER
MASSACHUSETTS
Marshall arrived in Worcester where he met Louis "Birdie" Munger, his new employer and manager.

Marshall, we are going to make you a household name. I got a steady job for you and I got some races all lined up.

BICYCLE WAREHOUSE
Marshall worked as a manager in Munger's warehouse.

During the day he worked in the warehouse.

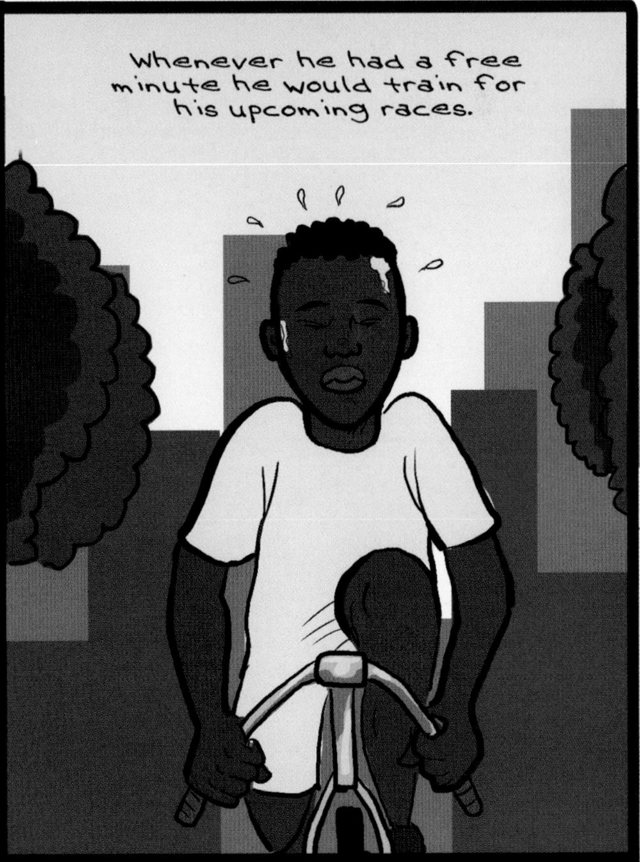
Whenever he had a free minute he would train for his upcoming races.

In his first professional race, it was clear right from the start...

DUST
...that Marshall would dominate.

CAW!
He was so fast that at one point he had lapped all the other competitors.

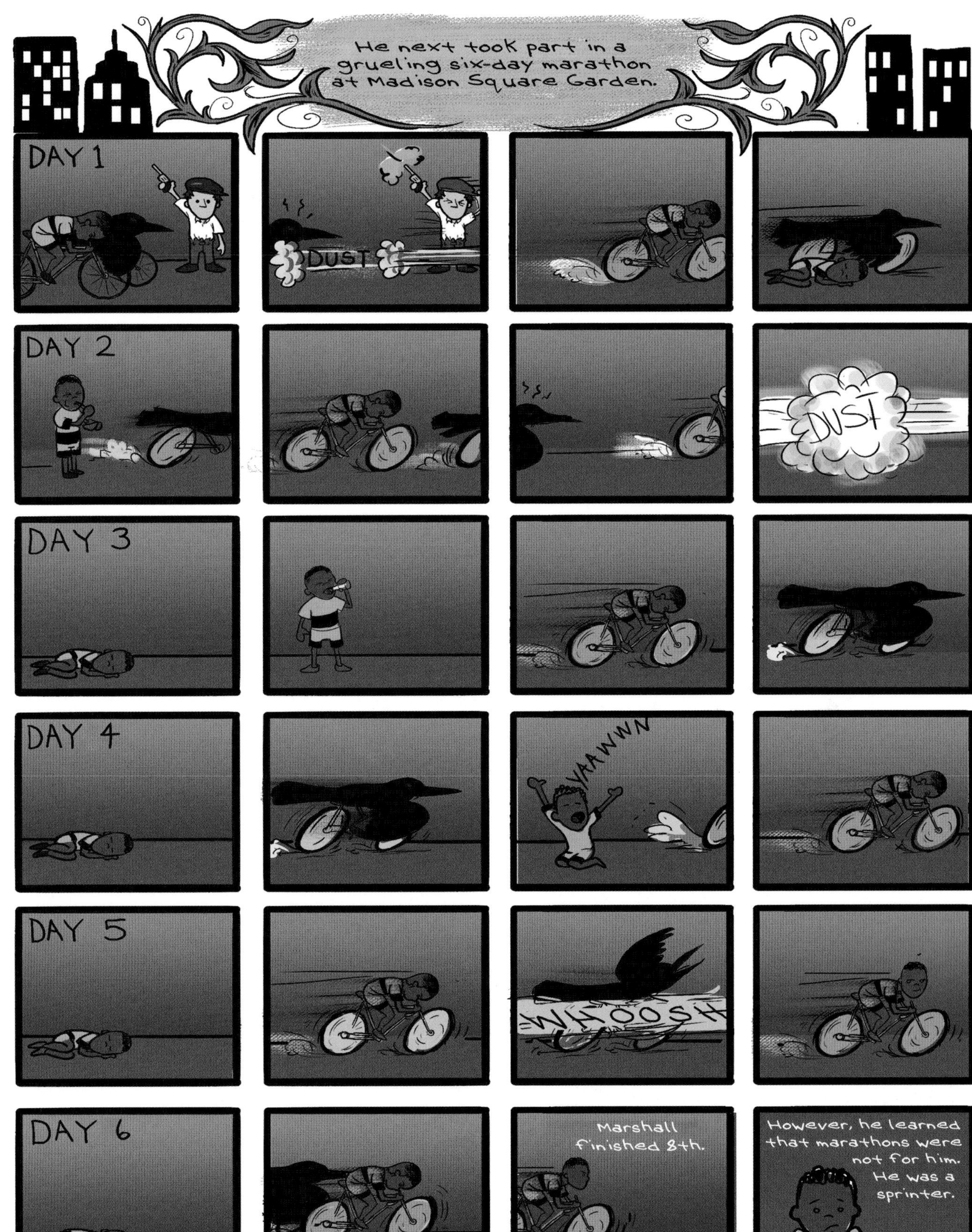
He next took part in a grueling six-day marathon at Madison Square Garden.
DAY 1
DUST
DAY 2
DUST
DAY 3
DAY 4
YAAWWN
DAY 5
WHOOSH
DAY 6
Marshall finished 8th.
However, he learned that marathons were not for him. He was a sprinter.
8

...even as Jim Crow nearly caught him in Boston.

7 WORLD RECORDS

However, Taylor's accomplishments began to pile up. By 1899, no one could deny he was the best in the world. Even the president was a fan.

World Champion

FIRST FAN!

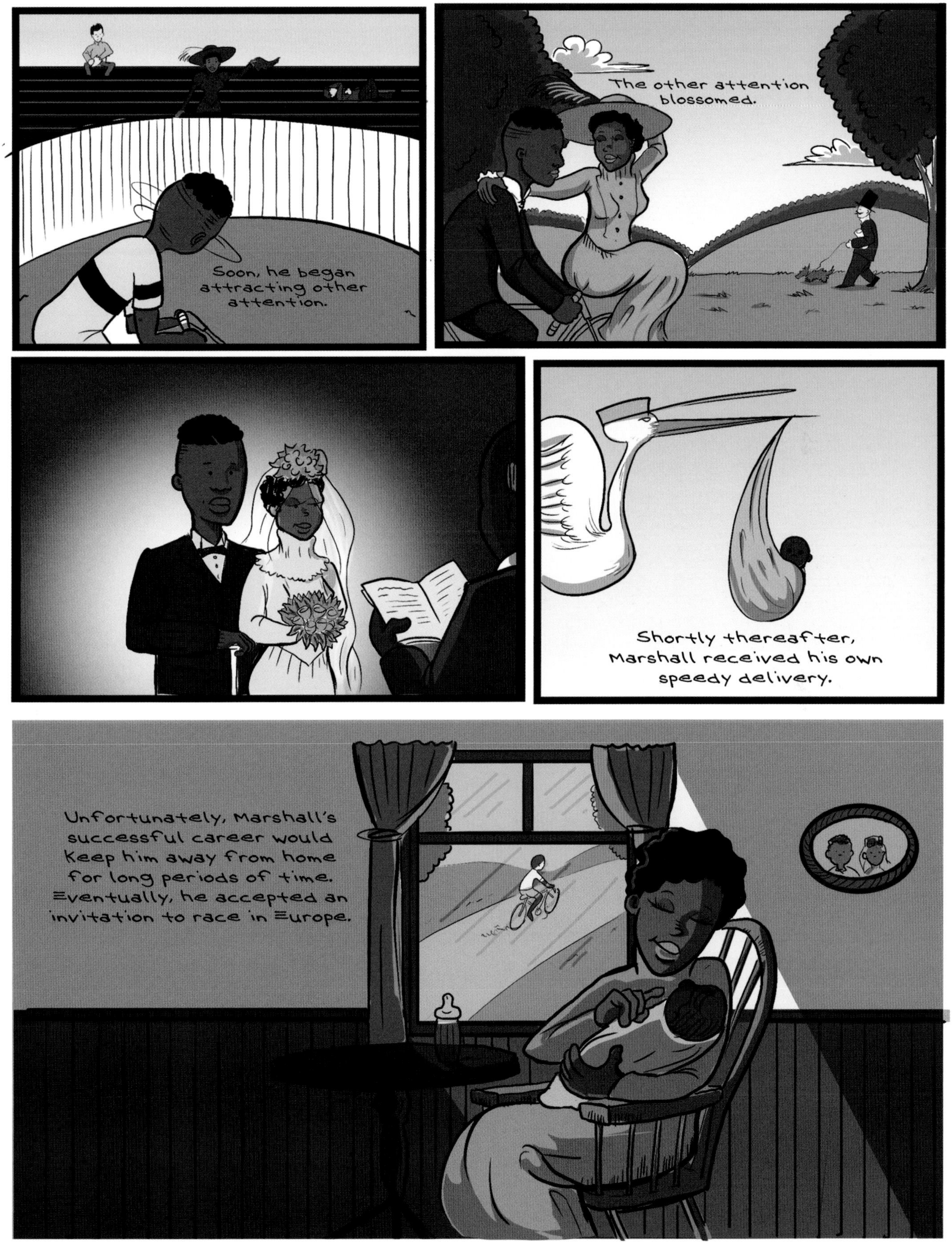

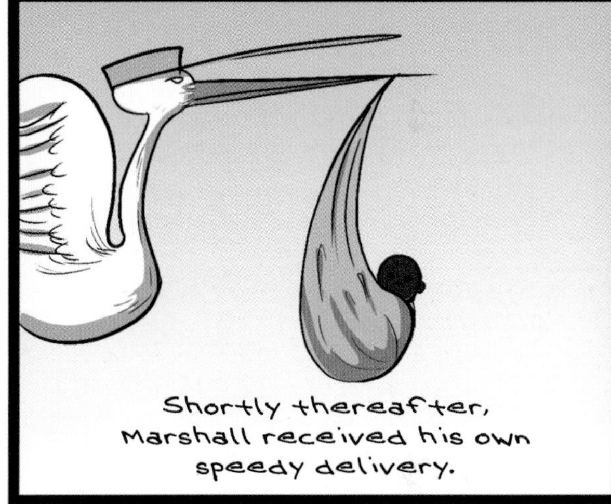

Soon, he began
attracting other

The other attention
blossomed.

Shortly thereafter,
Marshall received his own
speedy delivery.

Unfortunately, Marshall's successful career would keep him away from home for long periods of time. Eventually, he accepted an invitation to race in Europe.

GREAT
BRITAIN

FRA E

Marshall spent so much time away that it affected his marriage. His wife could take no more.

Marshall still won races as he got older, but not by the same margins.

In 1910, Marshall decided to call it quits and pursue other endeavors.
Racing has been good to me, but I am no longer able to perform at the same level. So as of today, I am retiring from the world of cycling.

Things were good for a while. Marshall had made a significant amount of money over the years.

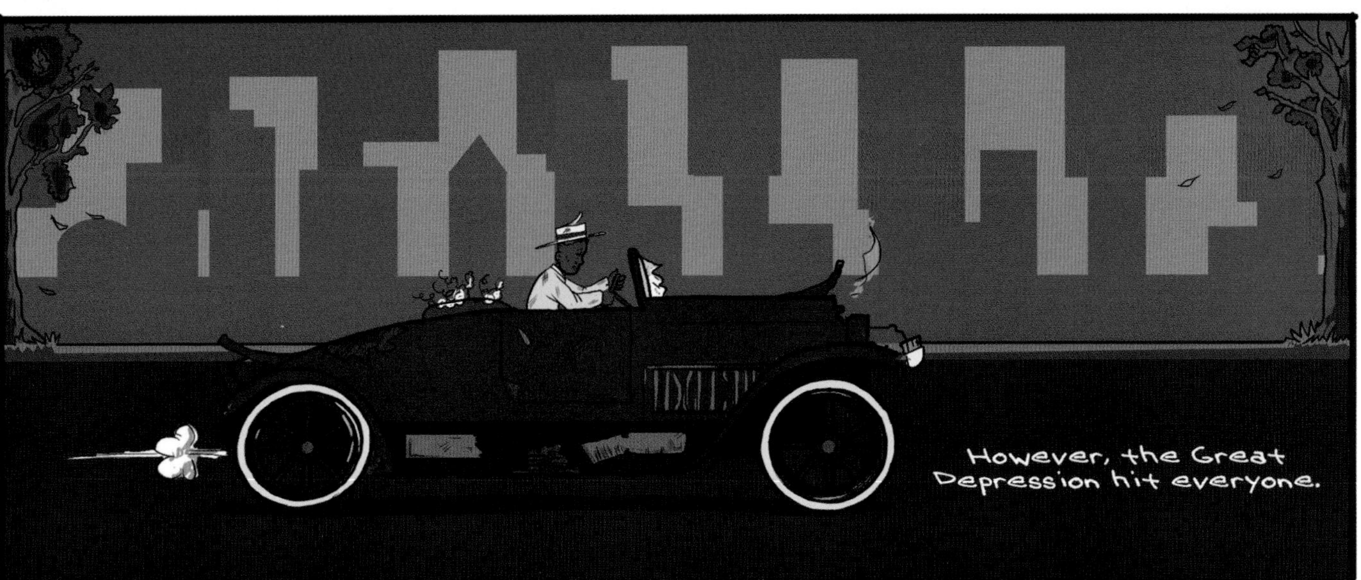
However, the Great Depression hit everyone.

Bad business deals and his self-published book left Marshall destitute.

Marshall ended up in Chicago.
HA Ha!

His old tricks could not help him.
SAD

Marshall spent the remainder of his days in the hospital charity ward.

He died in 1932 at the age of 54 and was buried in a pauper's unmarked grave in Chicago.

M.Taylor
b. unknown
d.1932

Some years later, a group of cyclists pooled their money and had Marshall moved to a proper resting place. In 2008, the city of Worcester, Massachusetts, Marshall's adopted hometown, erected a monument in his honor. The memorial recognizes the accomplishments of Marshall Taylor and is testament to how the Black Cyclone outran Jim Crow.

END

My Children, I take my pen in hand to rite you a few lines to let you know...

...I have not forgot you.

Two Letters

as Written by Spottswood Rice

I want you to be contented with
whatever may be your lots

but be assured

I will have you

if it cost me my life.
STATE LINE

On the 28th of the month
8 hundred White and 8 hundred
blacke soldiers
STATE LINE

expect to
start up the river
to Glasgow.

I expect to
be with them.

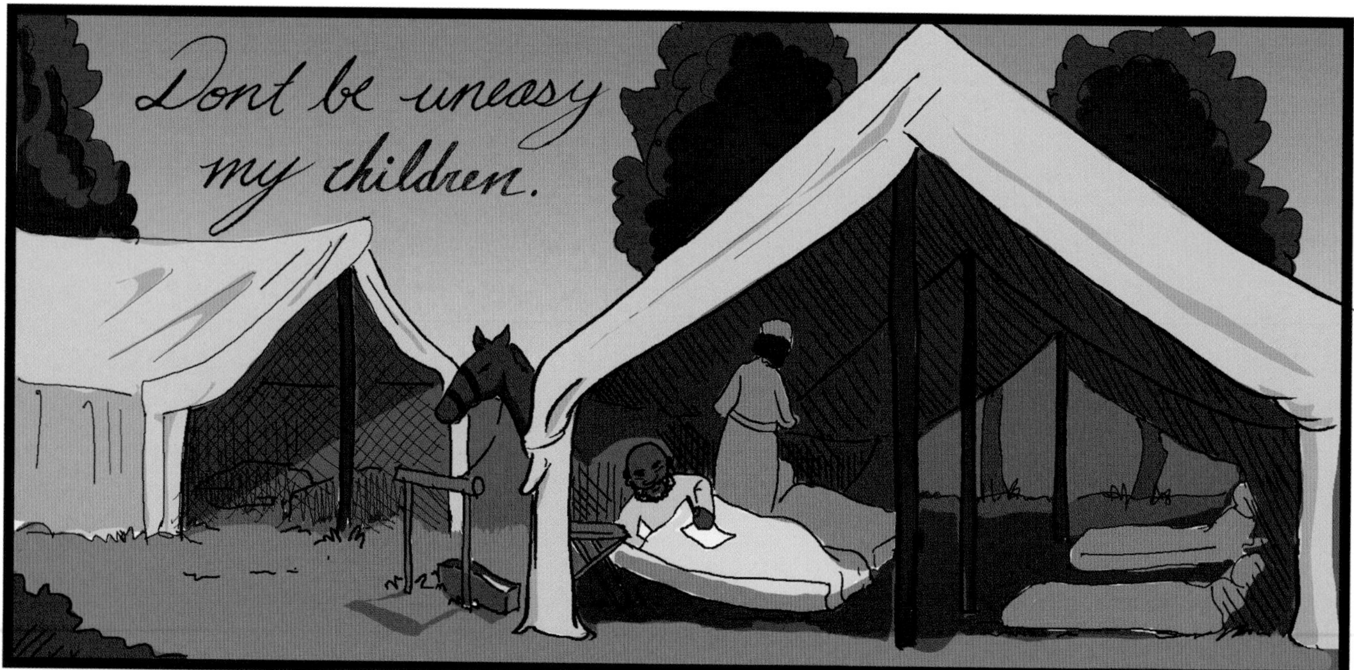
Dont be uneasy
my children.

I expect to have you.

Your Miss Kittey said
I tried to steal you.

God never intended for a man
to Steal his own flesh and blood.

If I had any Confidence in her I have none now.

And I want her to remember...

if she meets me with ten thousand soldiers

she will meet her enemy.

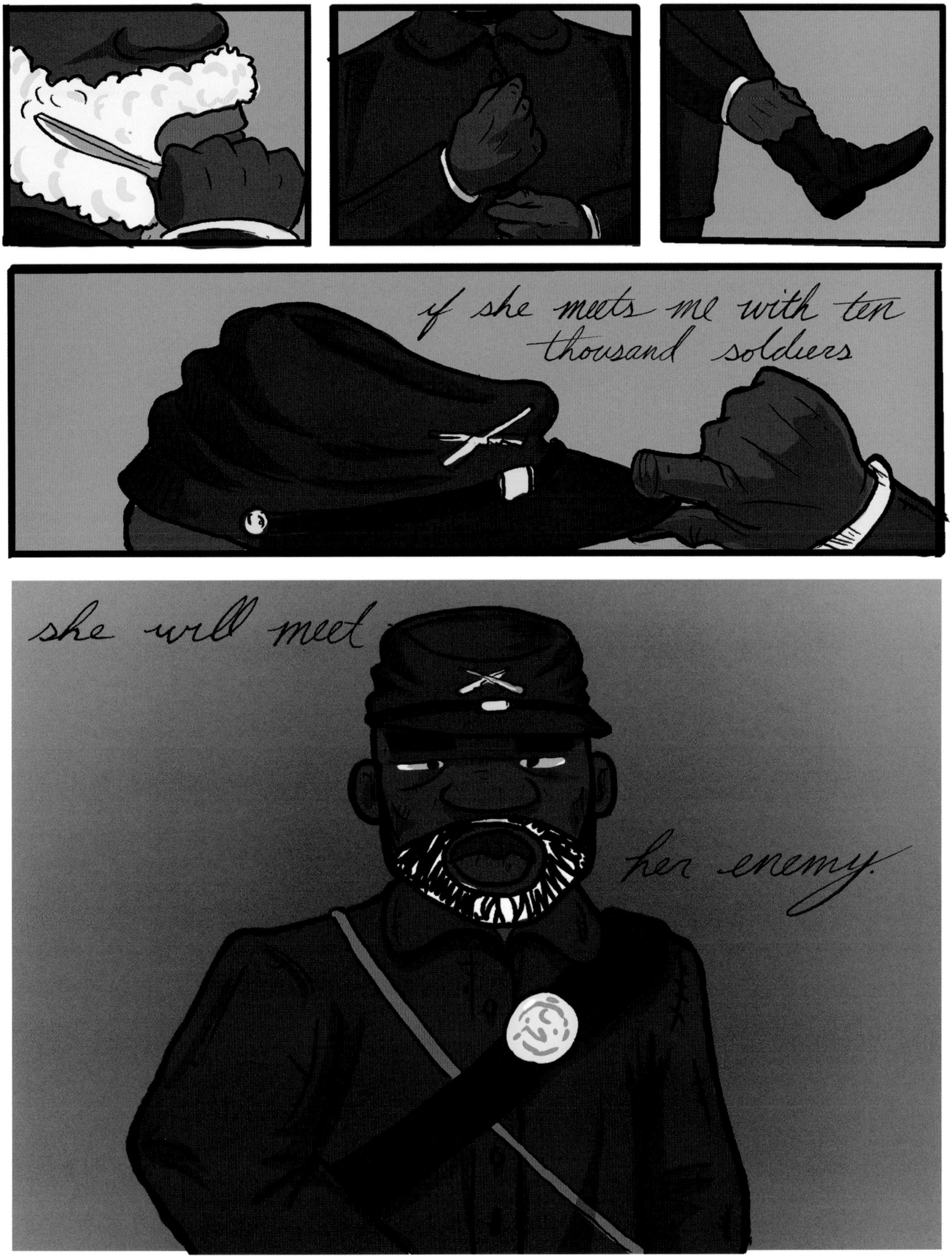

I have no sympathy for Slaveholders.

Give my love to all,

Spottswood Rice
POW

DAD

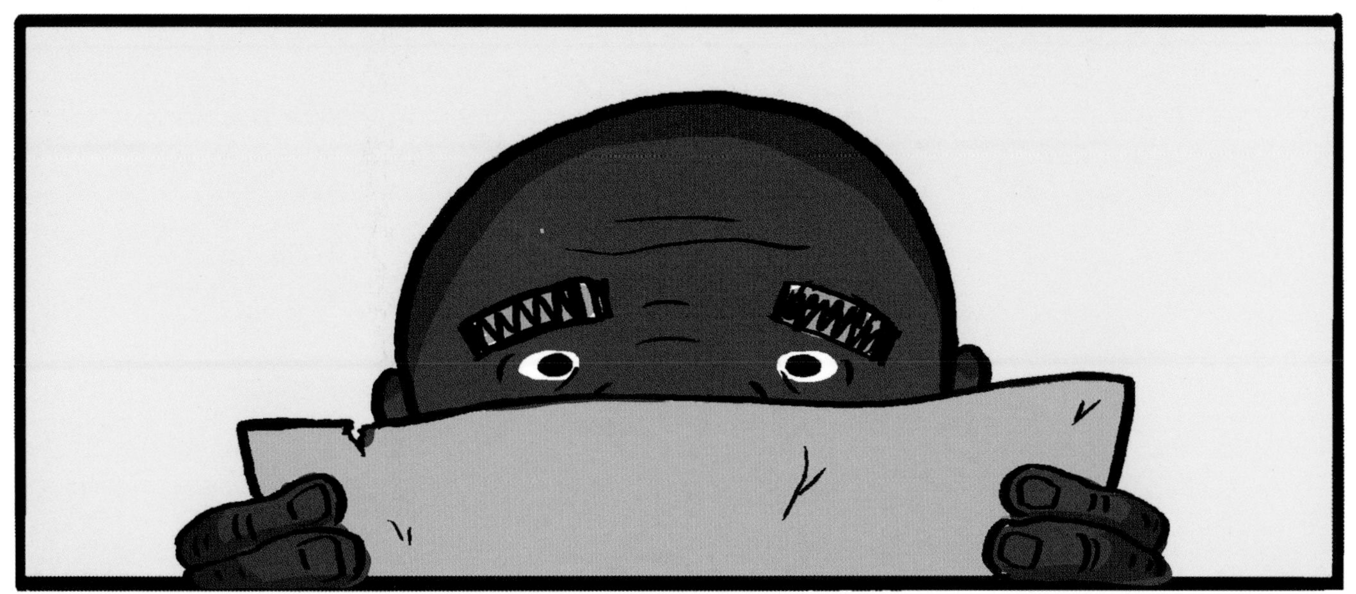

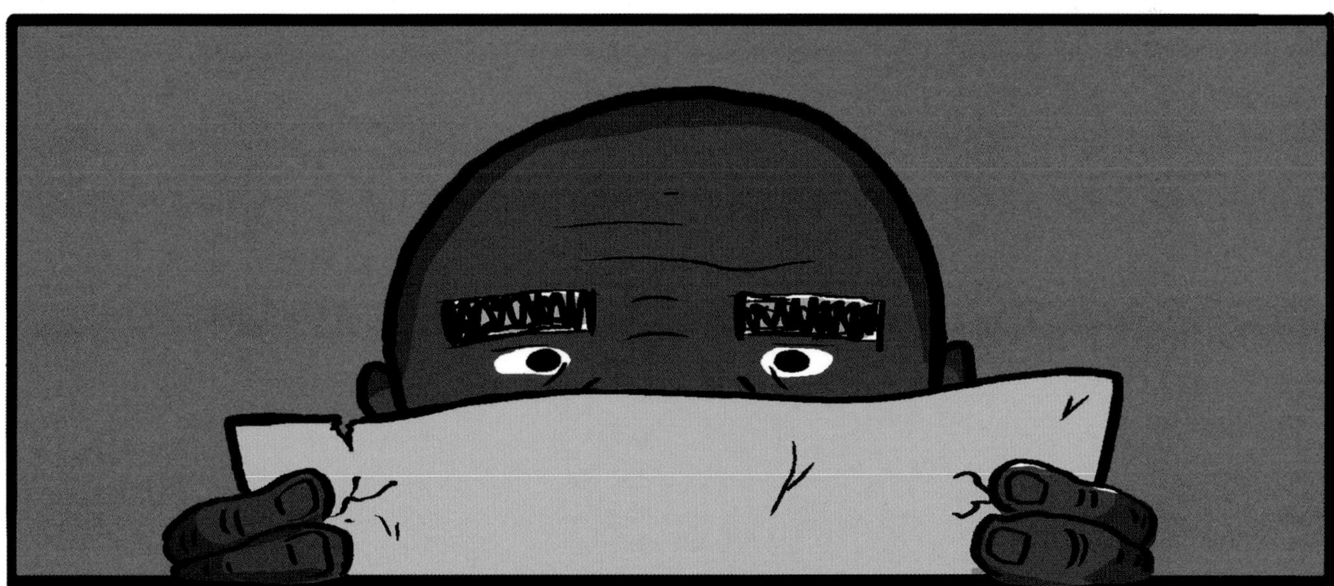

I received a leteter from Mary telling me that you say I tried to steal my Child

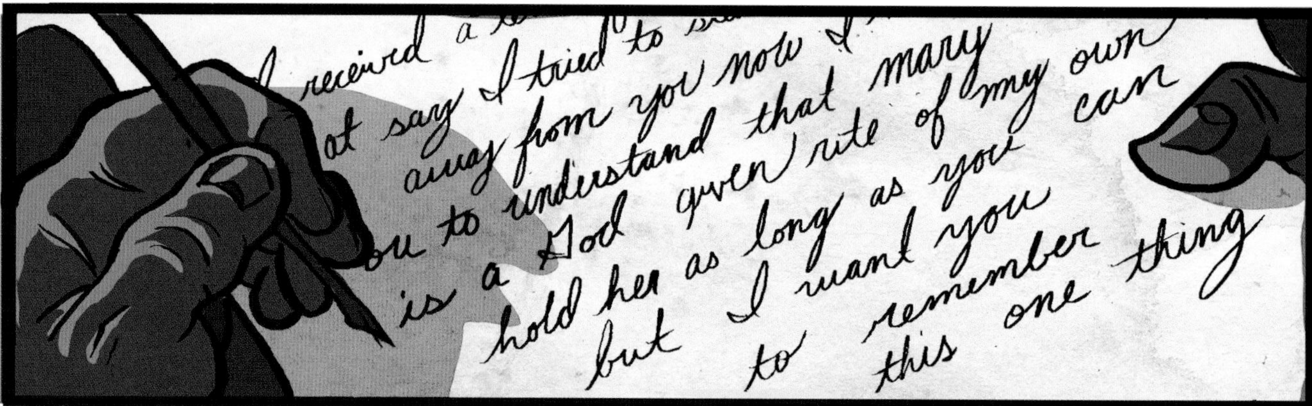
I received a
at say I tried to
away from you now I
ou to understand that mary
is a God given rite of my own
hold her as long as you can
but I want you
to remember
this one thing

the longor you keep my Child from me...

the longor you have to burn in hell and the quicer you'll get their.

SLAM

wo be to the
Copperhead rabbels
and to the Slaveholding
rabbels...

for we are making up
about one thousand blacke
troops. We don't expect
to leave them there
nor root nor branch.
Just hold on as long as
you can and the worse it
will be

Poof

I once offered to pay you $40...

for my own child.

BANG
BANG
BANG

I am glad now that you did not accept.

The day that we enter Glasgow I want you to understand Kitty Diggs...

my child is
my own.

you call my child...

property.

I have no fear about getting Mary out of your hands.

...And that's how my daddy, Spottswood Rice, came and took me from slavery all those years ago.

Indian Territory, circa 1890s

Hey, you lazy darky! Take my horse, boy.

I am talking to you! Take my horse!

ANSWER ME BOY!

Hoochk
Choo

Don't matter if you dumb or not. You better water my horse, else I'ma whip you like I bought and paid for you!

WANT'ED
REWARD
WANT'ED
REWARD

You're in my seat. I reckon you better move your Injun behind.
Excuse me, boss. About your horse.
What's with you people today? Do you hear me?
Maybe we should settle this outside like real men.
Maybe you should see about that.
Sir?
WHAT?!

I am afraid that I can't water your horse. You are wanted for horse theft and stagecoach robbery. I'm Bass Reeves, deputy U.S. marshal. I'm here to take you in.

You can't be going 'round snatching up white folks.

Yes, I can.
First, you take my partner, send him off with that Injun. Then you tie me to this darky. You better start answering me, boy!
Ain't no use.

What do you know that I don't, boy?
I know he won't answer and you won't get away.

You just got caught by one of the greatest deputy U.S. marshals there is. The legendary...
BASS REEVES
LAWMAN

Bass Reeves was born in Arkansas in 1838. His family was owned by farmer and future Confederate soldier George Reeves.

As a boy, Reeves was a deadeye-a crack shot with a rifle. His master soon developed a plan.

You about to make me some money, boy.

Ready, aim...

...FIRE!
POW

Bass was really good.

Bass grew up winning competition after competition.
He also grew up big, so George Reeves kept him as a manservant.

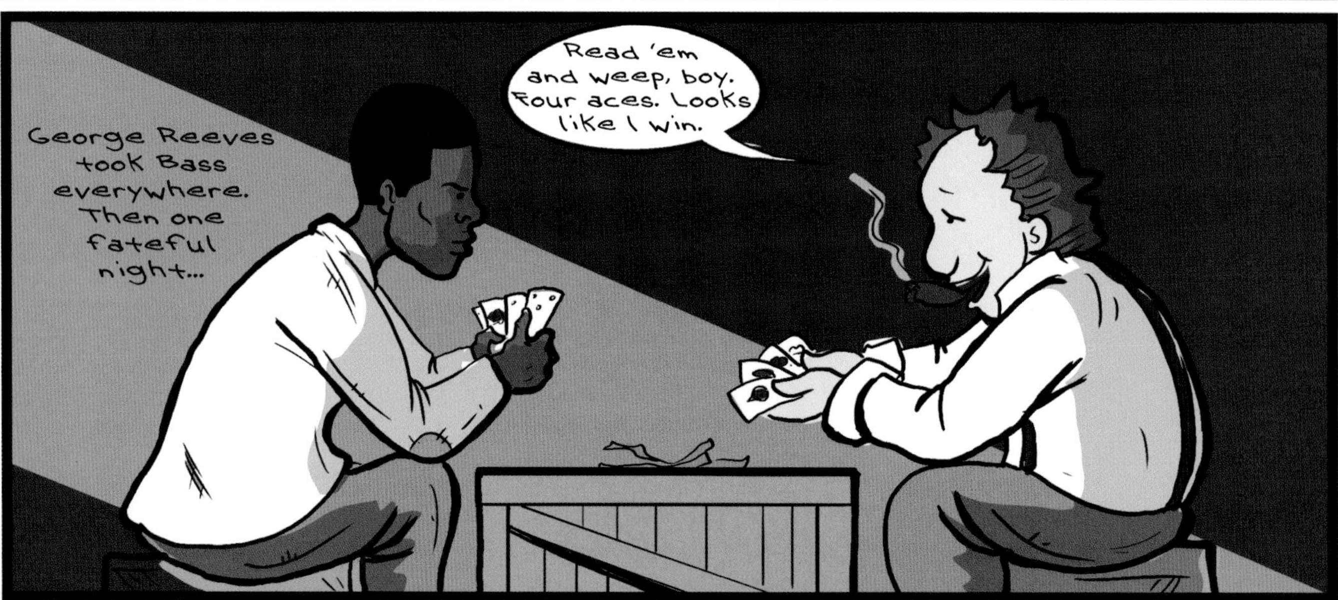
George Reeves took Bass everywhere. Then one fateful night...
Read 'em and weep, boy. Four aces. Looks like I win.

You can't have four aces, because I have one in my hand.
You are confused. You slaves ain't too bright.

You're a LOUSY CHEAT!

You just made the biggest mistake of your sorry life.

You better run, boy! 'Cause when you stop you'll be dead!

Bass ran. He ran until he could run no more.

The tribe decided the right thing to do was to nurse Bass back to health.

Bass was awake, and after weeks spent recovering, he was ready to discover where he had landed.

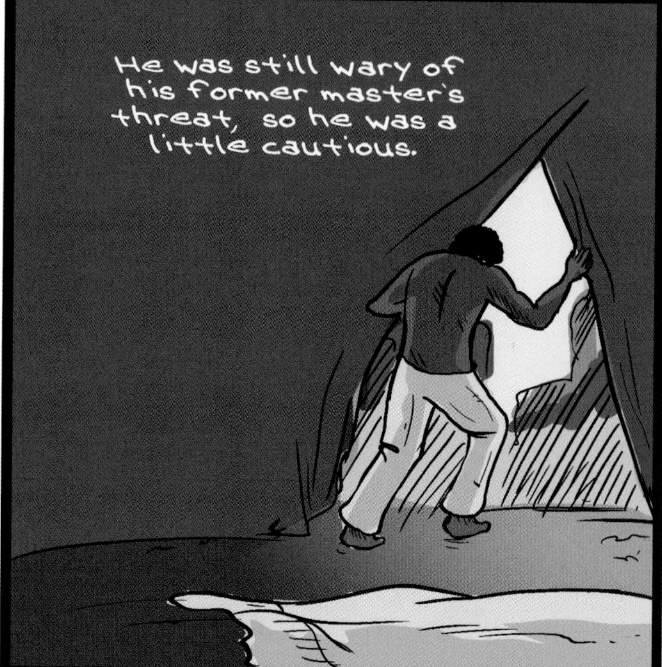

He was still wary of his former master's threat, so he was a little cautious.

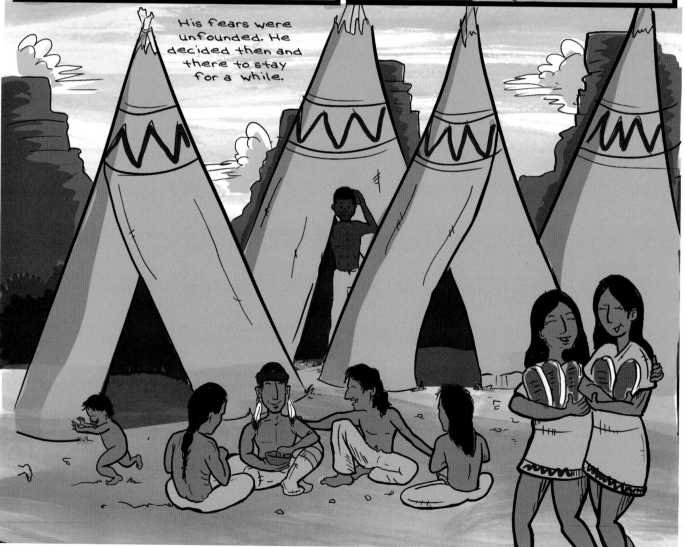

His fears were unfounded. He decided then and there to stay for a while.

After many years, Bass's old life was creeping toward his new life.

Hey there, stranger!!

I have never seen negroes with guns. What are you doing?

Where you been, boy? There is a war going on. We are fighting for our freedom.

Wait here. I will be right back.

<I have to go. My people need me.>

<You do what you must. >

If you dont mind, I would like to lend a hand or gun.
Welcome to the Union Army!
Bass later settled outside Indian Territory.
He soon married...
He had a quiet, peaceful life.

Howdy, Mr. Reeves. I hear you're pretty good around Indian Territory. I wonder if you could help us U.S. marshals track some outlaws into the territories.
That shouldn't be a problem. Let's head out there in the morning.

The next day...

<It is good to see you, brother. Have you seen any strangers?>
<It has been awhile, brother. And yes, there have been troublemakers.>

<He has been down there a few weeks now.>

You're surrounded. Nothing you can do. Turn yourself in peacefully or we will come in after you.

Bass was very good at helping the marshals.

Sir, I think I found a man for your new deputy program.
Judge Isaac Parker, "the Hanging Judge," presided over U.S. Western District Court. He wanted to deputize some black peace officers.

What are you waiting for, boy? Get over there and bring him!
Indians did not trust white officers because so many outlaws were white. Judge Parker thought they might trust black officers.

Judge Parker wants a word with you, Bass.

Bass, we need good men to fight lawlessness in the territories. You were a big help and I want you to be a deputy U.S. marshal.

Do you, Bass Reeves, swear before God, to uphold and serve the laws established to protect and govern the Federal Territories of the Western District of the United States of America?

I SWEAR.

Among Reeves's many challenges was the fact that he could not read.
Here is your warrant, Deputy.

Could you read it to me?
I sure can, Deputy Reeves.

He would memorize the details and ride off into the badlands.

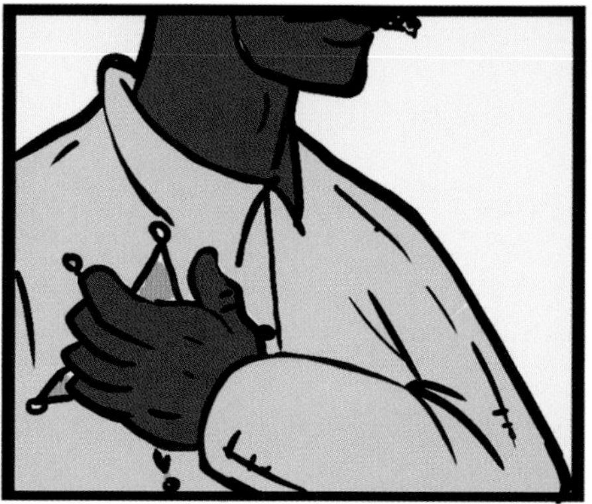

On one occasion, he dressed as an outlaw and walked 27 miles to the known hideout of two outlaws.

They were out when he arrived, so he told their mother that he was also running from the law.

When the outlaws arrived home, their mother explained the situation.

They decided that Bass could stay the night and in the morning could ride out with them.

Bass waited until the wee hours of the morning.

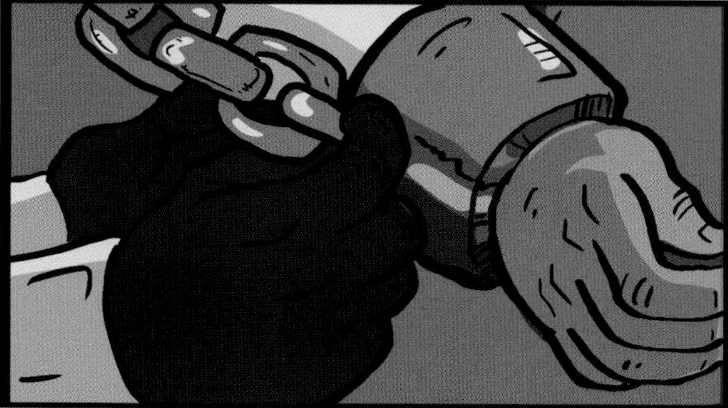

Wakey wakey, sleepyheads. You boys got a date with the hanging judge for the crime of murder.

Their mother was so furious that she followed halfway, yelling curse words at ole Bass the whole time.
#@*?!! =%#$!
Get moving.

On another occasion, some bandits TRIED to ambush the lawman.
MISS
They did not try hard enough.

On other occasions, Bass did the ambushing.
Hold it right there!
No more stagecoach and bank robbing for you.
Bass always got his man.
Excuse me, but are you that famous bank robber?
Who's asking ?
Bass Reeves, deputy U.S. Marshal.
#@*%!
Stupid men often thought that they could choose an easier way of escape.
POW
Turns out it always was harder.

Come in and state your business. I ain't got all day.
NEWS
WANTED
If you're the sheriff, I have come to turn myself in to you.
WANTED
My name is Belle Starr, and I'm a wanted outlaw. I was told that ole Bass Reeves was looking for me, and I ain't gonna have him hauling me all over the creation. Shoot, he would've caught me anyway soon enough.

He was right good with a pistol. Better with a rifle. Them bank robbers did not stand a chance. He left this silver coin behind.
Folks began to tell stories about Bass.

He rode a large black horse. He was polite and a sharp dresser. He did not say his name but left a silver coin.

The white men had stolen my horse, but a buffalo soldier came and got my horse back. He left this silver coin.

They were about to rob the coach I was in, when all of a sudden a negro with a gun saved the day. He left this silver coin.
He couldn't read so he always left a silver coin behind as a calling card.

You just been caught by the greatest lawman in the West.

How you know all this stuff? You run his fan club?

WYOMING TERRITORY
NEBRASKA
IOWA
COLORADO
KANSAS
MISSOURI
OKLAHOMA TERRITORY
INDIAN TERRITORY
ARKANSAS
The West changed from then on. Lawmen like my father were no longer needed as the lawlessness that had overcome the territories declined. Those crimes became statistics, and later the West became the Old West, and the outlaws and lawmen became legends.

I was pardoned for my crimes and set free.

By then my father had truly become history.

REEVES

My father served the U.S.
marshals for 30 years, capturing
3,000 outlaws in that time.

After retiring he became a
police officer — in those times
a much easier line of work.

He walked the beat for the
rest of his days.

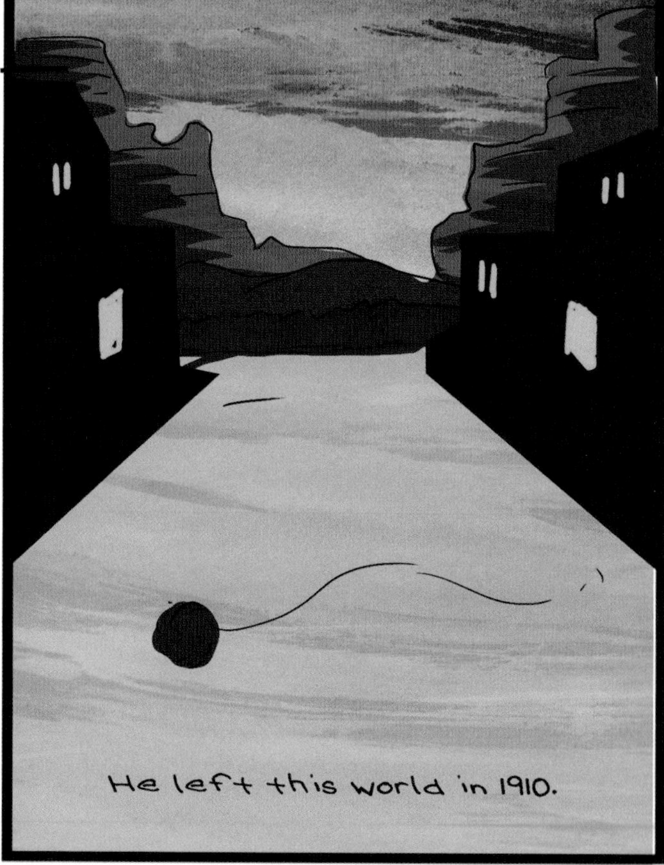
He left this world in 1910.

Some years later I heard a radio program about a masked lawman in the Old West. He fought crime and kept the peace...

It sounded familiar.

Did You Know?

Out-of-the-Box Thinking: Henry "Box" Brown

The Underground Railroad was a network of secret routes leading from slavery in the South to freedom in the North. Along the route "stationmasters" and "conductors" helped escaping slaves move from one safe place to another until they were free. Henry "Box" Brown found one of the more unusual modes of hiding on the way to freedom.

Nothing up my sleeve.

Richard Potter's Greatest Illusion

By 1906, Richard Potter was mostly forgotten. Then, Harry Houdini ran an ad asking for information on "old time magicians." Here is part of one response to the ad that Houdini published in his magazine: "[Potter] threw up a ball of yarn and he and his wife "climbed upon it and vanished in the air..." – it was the Indian rope trick.

IN!
IN!
IN!

Harry "Bucky" Lew: Original Baller

In 1950, the Boston Celtics drafted the first African American basketball player, Chuck Cooper. When questioned about the choice, one of the team's owners reportedly replied, "I don't give a damn whether he's striped, plaid, or polka dot!"

Theophilus Thompson: From Slave to Chess Master

Chess has been around for at least 1,500 years, so, naturally, the game has seen lots of "firsts." One of the most exciting of these happened in 1978, when Nona Gaprindashvili became the first woman ever to become a chess Grandmaster – the highest title possible for modern chess players.

The Shame

Before being forced from their homes in 1912, the people of Malaga Island struggled to eke out a living. The soil was too poor to farm, so many relied on trapping lobsters, hooking cod, or digging clams, while others traveled to the mainland to work as laborers.

The Noyes Academy

Before the Civil War, in many places it was against the law to educate African Americans. By 1835 – the year the Noyes Academy was founded – almost all of the Southern states had outlawed education for slaves.

Marshall "Major" Taylor: The Black Cyclone

Today, it's common to see people doing "tricks" on BMX bikes that have been modified so riders can more easily do amazing stunts with them, like balancing at crazy angles and doing jumps. Now take a look at the bicycle "Major" Taylor used for his tricks!

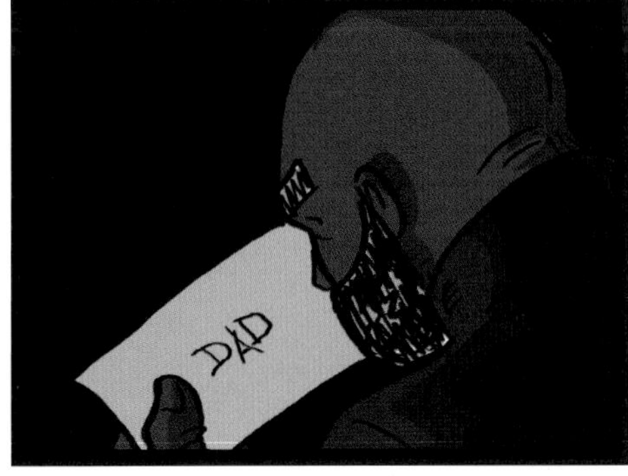

Two Letters, as Written by Spottswood Rice

During the Civil War, soldiers treasured their letters. Getting one, or having a letter reach its destination, was often nothing short of a miracle. Mail during that time was never a sure thing: not only were soldiers constantly on the move, mail was also often intercepted to learn the enemy's secrets.

Bass Reeves: Lawman

Bass Reeves encountered – and lived with – a number of different Native American tribes during his time in Indian Territory. In this story, rather than translate the languages he learned and focus on any one group's way of life, you'll see broad representations of both Native American pictographs and culture.

Bibliography

Out-of-the-Box Thinking: Henry "Box" Brown

- Appiah, Kwame Anthony, and Henry Louis Gates. *Africana: The Encyclopedia of the African and African American Experience*, Vol. 2, 2nd ed. New York: Basic Civitas Books, 1999.
- Appiah, Kwame Anthony, and Henry Louis Gates. *Africana: The Encyclopedia of the African and African American Experience*. Oxford, UK: Oxford University Press, 2005.
- Mahnken, Kevin. "This End Up: The Story of Henry Box Brown's Escape from Slavery." Humanities 34.3 (2013): 6. Art Full Text (H. W. Wilson). Web. Retrieved Oct. 13, 2012.
- Robbins, Hollis. "Fugitive Mail: The Deliverance of Henry 'Box' Brown and Antebellum Postal Politics." *American Studies* (00263079) 50.1/2 (2009): 5–25. Academic Search Premier. Web. Retrieved Dec. 7, 2012.

Harry "Bucky" Lew: Original Baller

- Ragsdale, Kathie Neff. "Bucky Lew Made Basketball History." *Eagle-Tribune* (North Andover, MA), Feb. 22, 2001.
- Robertson, Tatsha. "A Rare Lineage: A Black Family Boasts Early Mass. Roots." *Boston Globe*, Feb. 21, 1999.
- Wolff, Cynthia Griffin. "Passing Beyond the Middle Passage: Henry 'Box' Brown's Translations of Slavery." *Massachusetts Review* 37.1 (1996): 23. Academic Search Premier. Web. Retrieved June 7, 2013.

Richard Potter's Greatest Illusion

- Early America. Maps ETC. Florida Center for Instructional Technology. Retrieved Apr. 20, 2011, http://etc.usf.edu/maps/pages/2600/2685/2685.htm.
- Napoleonic Europe, 1799–1815. Maps ETC. Florida Center for Instructional Technology. Retrieved Apr. 20, 2011, http://etc.usf.edu/maps/pages/7800/7815/7815.htm.
- Robinson, Dennis. "America's First Black Magician, Richard Potter." African American Registry. Jan. 1, 2006. Seacoast, NH. Retrieved Sept. 1, 2011, http://www.aaregistry.org/historic_events/view/americas-first-black-magician-richard-potter.
- Samuel, Colleen Benham "BLACK Magic." *American Legacy: Celebrating African-American History & Culture* 7.1 (2001): 29. Academic Search Premier. Web. Retrieved June 7, 2013.

Theophilus Thompson: From Slave to Chess Master

- Brennan, Neil. "Theophilus Thompson – Master Emeritus." Feb. 1, 2006. *The Chess Drum*. Retrieved July 1, 2011, http://www.thechessdrum.net/drummajors/T_Thompson.html.
- "Chess." *Black Firsts: 4,000 Ground-Breaking and Pioneering Historical Events* (p. 672). Canton, MI: Visible Ink Press, 2003. Credo Reference. Web. Retrieved June 11, 2013.

The Shame

- Cover, Susan M. "Bill Aims to Protect Malaga's Descendants." *Portland Press Herald* (ME), Apr. 19, 2013: Newspaper Source. Web. Retrieved June 11, 2013.

- "Malaga Island – A Story Best Left Untold." Rob Rosenthal and Kate Philbrick, WMPG, and the Salt Institute. Radio documentary, WMPG Greater Portland Community Radio, 2009.
- Woodard, Colin. Opinion: "Malaga Island: A Century of Shame." *Portland Press Herald* (ME), May 20, 2012: Newspaper Source. Web. Retrieved June 11, 2013.

The Noyes Academy

- Haasâ, Genevieve. "The Brief, but Courageous Life of Noyes Academy." Home/Dartmouth College. Dec. 5, 2005. Web. Retrieved Feb. 11, 2013, http://www.dartmouth.edu/~dartlife/archives/15-5/noyes.html.
- Irvine, Russell W., and Donna Zani Dunkerton. "The Noyes Academy, 1834–35: The Road to the Oberlin Collegiate Institute and the Higher Education of African Americans in the Nineteenth Century." *Western Journal of Black Studies* 22.4 (1998): 260. Academic Search Premier. Web. Retrieved July 1, 2013.
- Williams, Jasmine K. "The Life of the Rev. Alexander Crummell." *New York Amsterdam News*, Jan. 26, 2012: 28. Academic Search Premier. Web. Retrieved June 11, 2013.

Marshall "Major" Taylor: The Black Cyclone

- Henry, Tanu T. "A Speedster on Two Wheels." *Footsteps* 7.3 (2005): 22. MasterFILE Premier. Web. Retrieved March 1, 2013.
- Kifer, Ken. "Major Taylor – A Forgotten Hero." Jan. 1, 2002. Major Taylor Association. Retrieved Nov. 1, 2012, http://www.majortaylorassociation.org/Kifer.htm.
- Historical Atlas of Europe (June 1, 1912). OMNIATLAS. Retrieved Apr. 15, 2013, http://maps.omniatlas.com/europe/.

Two Letters, as Written by Spottswood Rice

- Walton-Raji, Angela Y. "The Words, Actions and Life of Spottswood Rice – Freedom Fighter (Parts 1 and 2)." *The USCT Chronicle*, Mar. 12, 2012. Retrieved June 12, 2012, http://usctchronicle.blogspot.com/2012/03/words-actions-and-life-of-spottswood.html.

Bass Reeves: Lawman

- Burton, Art T. *Black Gun, Silver Star: The Life and Legend of Frontier Marshal Bass Reeves.* Lincoln: University of Nebraska Press, 2006.
- Burton, Art T. "Lawman Legend Bass Reeves: The Invincible Man Hunter." *Wild West* 19.5 (2007): 50. MasterFILE Premier. Web. Retrieved June 12, 2013.
- "Pictographs." Native Indian Tribes. Retrieved Nov. 26, 2013, http://www.warpaths2peacepipes.com/native-indian-art/pictographs.htm.
- "Social Studies: Printables Native American Picture Writing." Teacher Vision. Family Education Network. Oct. 1, 2013. Retrieved Nov. 24, 2013, https://www.teachervision.com/native-american-history/printable/7198.html?detoured=1.
- Soodalter, Ron. "Long Arm of the Father." *Oklahoma Today* 62.6 (2012): 38. MasterFILE Premier. Web. Retrieved June 12, 2013.

Joel Christian Gill

is the chairman, CEO, president, director of development, majority and minority stockholder, manager, co-manager, regional manager, assistant to the regional manager, receptionist, senior black correspondent, and janitor of Strange Fruit Comics. In his spare time he is the Associate Dean of Student Affairs at the New Hampshire Institute of Art and member of the Boston Comics Roundtable. He received his MFA from Boston University and a BA from Roanoke College. His secret lair is behind a secret panel in the kitchen of his house (sold separately) in New Boston, New Hampshire, where he lives with his wife, four children, talking dog, and two psychic cats.

He is not currently in a bad mood.

Thank You

(noun: an expression used to convey gratitude)

There were a lot of people who helped me in ways great and small but here are a few: Brian Sieveking, Scott Hardwig, Bill White, John Walker, and Ronda Philips. The librarians at the New Hampshire Institute of Art and the Boston Comics Roundtable helped with research and critique along the way.

Thank you to all the friends and family (especially my children, Victoria, Aerial, Mary Catherine, and Christian) who listened to me blab on about obscure history.

Most of all, thank you, April. You saved my life.

Strange Fruit is an evocative and richly illustrated tour through the shadowed corners of Black History. Gill shares these nine stories simply and with deep thoughtfulness and reverence to voices that – the reader will quickly be convinced – need to be heard.

Andrew Aydin
Author, with Rep. John Lewis,
of *March: Book One*

These offbeat stories of heretofore-obscure African American pioneers are filled with heartbreak and triumph. Without whitewashing the realities of slavery and racism, *Strange Fruit* has a wry, welcoming tone — much aided by Gill's dynamic, inventive storytelling. After reading about such real American heroes as chess master Theophilus Thompson, bicycling champion Marshall "Major" Taylor, and lawman Bass Reeves, I'm eager to learn more!

Josh Neufeld
writer/illustrator of
*A.D.: New Orleans
After the Deluge*

By the time I finished reading *Strange Fruit*, I thought, let the comic-book sellers have their mythic superheroes; through Joel Christian Gill, we can have our own. But, instead of flying around in capes or spinning webs, the superheroes in *Strange Fruit* are extraordinary-ordinary black folks making 'a way out of no way.' The difference: they really lived.

Dr. Henry Louis Gates, Jr.
Alphonse Fletcher
University Professor,
Harvard University